For the Glory of God

Laura Crossgrove Baer

A CLOSER LOOK

Pain, Suffering And
Healing . . . What Does
The Bible Say?

BY LAURA CROSSGROVE BAER

Fairway Press
Lima, Ohio

A CLOSER LOOK

FIRST EDITION
Copyright © 1992 by
Laura Crossgrove Baer

7947 / ISBN 1-55673-499-9   PRINTED IN U.S.A.

Dedicated to our Bible study group: Judy B. and Judy K., Jennie, Chris, Claudia, Sandy, Janie.

Special thanks to Ellen and Evelyn who called often to encourage me to write a book.

To Lucille, Sandy and Ruth for typing the first drafts.

To Ruth for proofreading.

To Vicki for initial advice and encouragement.

Special thanks to my daughter, Judy Kulp, for illustrations and writing on divider pages, and who did so many things that I was unable to do and supported me all the way to the publisher; to my husband, Clarence; to my sons, Joe, John, Nathan and Mark; to their wives, Joan, Cathi and Judy, and the grandchildren, for the very best care while I was confined and engrossed in writing and getting well; to Myrtie for watering plants; to Barb for the good nursing care; to all who gave of their time to: pray for me, cook or bring food, send cards, visit, or just to love me.

To the Glory of Jesus Christ Our Lord!

Table Of Contents

PART I
A Touch Of Reality

I want my brothers and sisters in Christ who are hurting to be able to experience this same atmosphere of freedom and acceptance I experienced.

A Touch Of Reality

This book on healing wholeness is the result of questions that were asked of me when I was confined to bed for two and one-half years. I believe the best way to answer such legitimate questions is with Biblical support.

The Scriptures have something to say concerning the life of a person and what he believes. We must not shut out Christ Jesus from any area of our lives as if He is not interested. He and the Word agree and stand behind all healing whether it happens with or without the aid of the medical profession. He is interested in the wholeness of a person, both body and soul.

A follower of Jesus must look at the healing miracles of Jesus in the context of both the Old and New Testaments of the Bible. The Old is past and we are in the second advent period waiting for the second coming of Jesus, which will be the end time. To expect the healing of all sickness and disease right now is to look for the end before the end. It is not always easy to find a balance here and now unless we look into God's Word.

When the healing question was raised and discussed in our Bible study group, there was a desire to have our discussions and thoughts in writing. I considered it a challenge. Physically, I was limited. I knew there were examples with Biblical support, but they needed to be drawn together and put on paper in simple, everyday, understandable language.

What I first wrote was more of an outline for study and reference, but by including explanations and more direct verses from the scriptures, it has become a work like none that I have ever seen before. I pray it will be most helpful to anyone who reads it.

I did not think it was necessary to write about my own experience of pain and healing. I wanted the study to be read and used as a guide by itself. I have been advised, however, that it would be helpful to include my own experience.

For only one reason do I write this; that is so that our Almighty Father will receive glory and I will have testified of the one and only exalted Son of God Jesus Christ Our Savior and Redeemer. Only by His grace and mercy am I able to testify of His great love that emanates and flows from an omnipotent God continually.

People often like to read about dramatic or sensational healings. My experience was not like what is written about by most persons. People are not alike, so experiences differ.

I did not have a battle with the Lord, an experience talked about by many persons. I did not have a battle with myself, trying to figure out the wrongs or rights and blaming God unjustly. What happened to me was part of normal Christian living. I had the assurance that I was abiding in Christ as a loved, forgiven believer. It is the right and privilege of every Christian believer to have this assurance.

I loved the Lord. My attachment to Him was real and His love for me was constant.

We sometimes hear people say, "Sure, we love the Lord and He loves us. He loves all people." Is His love actually real to them? We also hear, "I suppose He loves me." That statement does not sound confident. 1 John 4:19 says, "We love Him because He first loved us." Read the whole chapter and include chapter five.

Romans 8:16 says, "The Spirit Himself testifies with our spirit that we are God's children."

The Father God and the Son loved me so much that even before I was born, a plan was formulated that I could live with love, free and happy here on earth. Free and yet accountable. Free from the fear of death without mercy and free from the fear of fear.

God gives His children a spirit of love. The Son loved me so much that in obedience to the Father He came to earth to be like one of us earth creatures. He did this so that He could die in my (our) place. Now I can live a liberated life through Him. That is love.

I love Him in return. That means I have accepted His plan for my life. I have made a choice. By faith I abide in Him and His Word and allow His Spirit to direct my ways. When we have this assurance we can do anything the Lord requires or allows for us because it brings peace. We really have an opportunity to live like Jesus lived when we are well or sick. The challenge is in trying to learn the truth and gain the victory.

My particular experience began one October night in 1977. Everything was ready for our family to cook apple butter the following day at our 1890s farm-lifestyle local museum. As I retired for the night, the muscles in my left arm between the elbow and the shoulder were struck with an excruciating pain. Like a bolt of lightning, it came suddenly and severely. It made no difference how I tried to relieve it, the pain persisted. My night's sleep was gone.

We went ahead with our plans the next day. My arm became no better. One week later my right arm was struck with the same sudden pain as my left arm had been. I had them checked by our family doctor who said, "It is probably arthritis. Take aspirin as needed." Sometime later, at a follow-up visit, he said, "It cannot be arthritis."

Then began testing with specialists and more specialists. My deltoid (shoulder) muscles were deteriorating, but no doctor understood why. I had no strength to lift even my own arms, but someone else could lift them and I had no pain. The doctors suspected muscular dystrophy or sclerosis, but the other symptoms were not present.

My elbows and hands at that time were in good condition, so I did what I could with my hands straight out in front of me. Combing my hair and putting on clothing were extremely difficult. My husband, Clarence, often had to help me. My button-up-the-front housecoat and I were almost inseparable.

I had been talking things over with the Lord and knew that He knew what was happening and that he cared. God calls His children to obedience and I was His child, so why not me? I was aware that in this body of mine lived His Spirit. I wanted to obey and keep His home livable and lovable.

If I were giving advice to anyone, I would like to say this . . . do as Job did concerning his children. Communicate with God daily and often. Keep yourself ready for His workings. Do not keep piling things up or putting them off for a more proper or convenient time, or when the preacher gives an invitation at church. That is important, too, but keep yourselves "prayed up." It makes it easier to listen and hear what He has for you. When we sit, when we stand, when we lie down, when we walk, we are the Lord's.

Meeting with specialists and having many kinds of tests was not easy, but necessary. They all shook their heads in puzzlement.

I was amused by one doctor's response. While I was resting and waiting on a cot in the hospital hallway, the doctor said, "Go home and come back. You are too sick to be examined." He had not tried.

I was stunned for a moment. It is good the Lord blessed me with a keen sense of humor. It reminded me of my son. When the day arrived for him to keep a doctor's appointment, he was not feeling well. He said, "Please call the doctor and cancel my appointment. I'm sick."

Another time I kept an appointment with the same specialist at his hospital office. I arrived early and reported to the desk nurse. She said it would be just a few minutes, so I waited with my husband in the lobby. We waited and waited. Waiting was difficult because I was not feeling well.

We checked with the nurses several times. They paged the doctor time after time, never getting a response. They began to show their concern. After all, we had driven forty miles and did have an appointment! The nurses decided he may have gone to another office and telephoned to check. Yes, he was there. We drove several blocks to the second office after waiting about two hours at the first. The nurses were as puzzled and upset as we were.

A surprised looking doctor faced me in his office and went through the same routine as usual, tapping my knees and elbows for reflexes and really explaining nothing. This particular day, after he had finished tapping, laid down his mallet and was half way out of the door without saying one word to me, my anger was stirred!

"Doctor, if you do not want me for a patient, please just tell me!" I said. Startled, he turned around and said, "I don't know what to do." So that was it! Finally it was out! I appreciated his honest answer and suddenly felt sorry for him. It would be difficult and maybe frustrating for a professional person to say what he said. They, too, are human just like me.

He suggested it would be good to go to a larger clinic. The nearest bigger clinic was 150 miles away, but we made arrangements to go. I had already been at several clinics and offices in the nearest city, forty miles from our farm. I did not look forward to more probes and grams.

My first visit to the larger clinic was in early autumn of 1978. We enjoyed the scenery as we drove the 150 miles.

I first saw neurologists who said I did not need them. The rheumatologists consulted for some time and said my problem appeared to be adhesive capsulitis and poly myalgia rheumatica.

Those words sounded big and the explanations were a bit vague as was our understanding of them. I was given the drug prednisone and instructions for physical therapy. The local hospital therapist and pharmacist gave us more information.

At first it seemed to help somewhat. It was really hard to tell. In just a short time though, I was definitely getting worse. My shoulders, knees and one elbow were affected with pains. My leg muscles began to hurt and I felt bad in general. The doctor said to continue the medication.

As time went by, my condition grew worse. I walked into the doctor's office and he said. "We've got to get you off that medication." After an examination, he said "I have nothing else to give you, so you had better stay on it." I really didn't want that 'something else.' All I wanted was relief. Then he gave me other medicine to try along with the prednisone, a form of cortisone. I tried nine different kinds, all of them with adverse effects on me.

13

Meanwhile, I tried to live as normally as possible and did what I was able to do at home. Some tasks did not get done. Life goes on anyway. I was told to keep on the move and move I did, slowly and painfully.

I was in touch with God all the time and people were praying for me. I started to use a cane, sometimes two. I learned that a walking stick is a good piece of equipment. No one should be hesitant about using one if necessary.

I was miserable. I was overweight. My skin was flushed and my system was toxic. I had to be careful not to rub my swollen knees together or the skin would break open.

In January of 1980 I spent twelve days at the clinic. The pains in my shoulders and legs were now called arthritis, but the pain in my upper arm muscles seemed to be unrelated. The doctors were puzzled. They continued to use the same diagnostic terms they used in the beginning. They knew I had many inflammations, but were unable to come to a full diagnosis.

One doctor said, "You are just not a textbook case."

It was obvious that the arthritis and the toxic condition were the resulting side effects of medication. One doctor confirmed this, explaining many of the different side effects. I asked if I could quit the prednisone and he replied, "If we did that, you would wish you were dead."

After a few more weeks my condition became even more alarming. By the time of our wedding anniversary, March 17, I had made the decision — no more medication. I was painfully aware of the doctor's caution about quitting.

In obedience to God's teaching in James 5, I had previously had a prayer of faith for healing and an anointing at church. This is a privilege not to be abused or taken lightly. I believed God would do what was best for my situation. He did. He had something for me to do which was not accomplished yet and was sustaining me in the process.

When a person has faith it brings responsibility. I had to be responsible because I had faith. I was aware of the danger in drug withdrawal and would not advise anyone to do it as I did unless there is prayer and much thought.

I told Clarence that if he could stand my moaning and groaning, I was going to quit the medication. I was careful, and in three weeks my withdrawal was past. I really had no extremely severe reactions, but I know the Lord sustained me.

The most frightening time was when I took a pill to help eliminate fluid build-up in tissue. That time I wanted Clarence to be nearby because I believed I might need help. I was shaky, my voice quivered and I felt flighty.

When my April appointment was due, I kept it as usual. The doctor thought I should see him again in six months. That sounded far off and miles away for the condition I was still in.

He said I could maybe reduce the dosage of the medication. I had already flushed the medication down the drain.

That may be foolish and unwise sometimes. It may not be right for someone else. In my case the medication seemed to work opposite from what it was intended.

I had already noticed a slight improvement during the three weeks since I had flushed the medication down the drain. I believed it would be better and safer to rid the shelf of all medication that had an adverse effect on me. For some people the same medication may be good. For me it was not.

The next week I began some new therapy treatments along with what I had been doing. If I as a Christian know there is a problem and do not do all I can to correct it, then I am not doing what is right physically or spiritually. We can sometimes function under these circumstances, but we cannot give of our best. Sometimes we know we could do better and do not. Shame on us because we act like children instead of adults, and we lose a blessing.

I needed better blood circulation to help my body rid itself of toxicity that made my eyes grayish-yellow and dull looking. The skin on my arms had become lifeless and dry. Something was very wrong.

Vitamins were no cure.

I learned from the therapist how very important the blood is to the human body. The comparison to the spiritual body, the church, is amazing. I realized it is a perfectly natural example of what the church is in its function.

Blood transports nurtrition and oxygen. Its composition can never be duplicated exactly. I believe I am glad about that. In the blood we have life and all other parts of the body depend on the blood for food as it circulates. An adult has five to six quarts of blood flowing through his veins at all times. The equivalent of six barrels of blood passes through the heart every hour. If the blood would not flow, the heart would have nothing to pump. Neither could we breathe if the blood stopped its function to the lungs. The brain could not function without it. Blood keeps the temperature of the body at 98.6 degrees.

There are four types of blood among all people everywhere, but the plasma of the blood is alike in all persons, "God has made of one blood all nations of men for to dwell on the face of the earth." Acts 17:26. (KJV) It is a marvelous thing the Lord has done for us. The blood cells are produced in the marrow of the bones and are so small that 60,000 of them will fit on a pin head.

Our blood is a lifeline. It is life-giving and life-keeping. If it does not flow we will die.

This is a good picture of how the spiritual church operates. The blood of Jesus is the lifeline for the church. When it flows properly the body parts work together in unity. When we rebel it is hindered. We need to ask ourselves, "Am I hindering the flow?" We need also to be honest about it when we ask.

I thought about the difference between the blood for a Christian and an unbeliever. To both it is just a sticky, red fluid that shows up when the skin gets pricked, but to a believer the blood also means life in Christ. His blood replaced mine when He died on the cross so I can live with love, too. We have two life cycles:

The physical is born to die.

The spiritual is born again to live anew.

Something was hindering the flow in my physical system. When through therapy the blood started to flow more properly in my veins, taking poisons with it, my body seemed to change again.

Time passed. I kept on with therapy until there was no further need for that particular kind. The doctor said he could do nothing more for me. He recommended I try elsewhere.

In February of 1981 I went to the well-known Mayo Clinic in Rochester, Minnesota. I believed I would not be doing right if I did not do all I could to keep my body in the best condition possible. It was not in good condition.

The doctor put me in a wheelchair immediately and said, "You should not be walking." I spent five days at Mayo Clinic as an outpatient. Tests were thorough and the final answer was, "The only thing that will help is complete bed rest, probably one year." By this time my body showed symptoms of over exertion and over medication. The doctor said, "No medication except ascriptin (anti-inflammatory)."

That was a change I welcomed. I have nothing against taking medication if necessary. That is part of God's provision, too. However, I already was suffering from overmedication and did not wish for more.

I have a thyroid condition which requires a daily intake of supplemental thyroid, but this had nothing to do with my other condition. Tests proved I was getting the correct thyroid dosage. That was an assurance that the Lord has an interest in our daily affairs, and that He will bring about in His time the plan of life he has purposed for each one of us.

At the birth of my first child, I was told that my pituitary and thyroid glands were damaged. Consequently, I need this daily thyroid supplement. When in 1963 we went to work in Puerto Rico I found at first only a synthetic thyroid supplement available. It was a critical time for me until the right supplement was found. In fact, one doctor said I should be dead. That was the third time I heard those same words.

It is so good to know that the Lord is interested in what happens to us. This is the way I felt when I was told to go to bed if I wanted help. I wanted help and the Lord knew it. He knows our innermost thoughts and I wanted to be obedient.

Going to bed was almost funny to us. I seldom had a cold or a headache. I had been hospitalized to have babies. I had

17

also had surgeries because of the fact that I was traveling through a world of decay and needed help sometimes. There was never a doubt in my mind as to who was traveling with me. I knew that together the Lord and I would go in the right direction. He gives His children this confidence that no matter what the detour is, we can move right along. This is normal Christian living.

At Mayo I was also told I had a chemical imbalance. My body normally produced a chemical to fight inflammation, but in my case, the doctor said, "There isn't enough to permit ordinary daily activity and still have any resistance against inflammation." His prescription was complete bed rest, so I came home and went to bed knowing that God does not give his children more than they can bear.

Some of my children lived far away, but I knew that I had a good family around me. It never occurred to me that my family would not help in whatever way they could. I felt that if no one panicked, we could manage. I did inquire for hired help, but none was available at that time. I was willing to go to a nursing home, but did not think it was necessary. I did not want to ask from the children more than they were able to do.

The thought of spending a year in bed, I believe, looked bigger to them than it did for me. I felt so bad physically and had been without proper sleep and rest for so many months that I really did not object, but I didn't want to be a burden to anyone. The children had their own families and work. I know it was difficult for them sometimes, but we stuck together and were all blessed.

While reading the Bible one evening, I tried to tune my thoughts with God's thoughts. The following poem came into my mind after reading Romans 11:33, 34 on May 12, 1981:

Who Can Know

Who can know the mind of God
by one mere dificulty along life's way?
Who can know the mind of God

18

by one small tear that drops, or
by one trill of laughter in the air?
Who can know the mind of God
by watching winds at work, or
birds that soar and wing amidst the clouds in space?
Who can know the mind of God
by all the stars that twinkle in their place?
Or sun and moon and galaxies unknown to his mortal
    race?
Who can know the mind of God
when thunder rolls and lightning streaks across the sky
Or when rivers swell with flooding rains
or gentle rains wash all the earth
to freshen dry parched fields?
Who can know the mind of God
by all the baser creatures He has made,
those that swim, those that roar,
those that moo or scratch,
and all the wiggly, crawly, creeping things?
Who can know the mind of God
in all the little seeds that sprout and grow to ripened grains
or trees burst forth with blossoms, then with fruits?
Who can know the mind of God
as seasons come and go and shall remain
so also — cold and heat and love and hate
as long as earth remains and man remains a man?
Who can know the mind of God
by looking to the hills, or
gazing at an endless stretch of desert sand?
Who can know the mind of God
who from the dust below our feet created He a man?
Who can know the mind of God
in all this big wide wonderful complex world?
Who can know the mind of God?
It is the One who traveled the way with man
so many years ago, and even now, before us.
It is the One who understands this mortal man
and how he lacks in balance and hopelessness within and
    by himself.
Who can know the mind of God?

It is the Lord who served us without measure on the cross
and in the tomb, then rose to heights,
to now impart to those who will —
a part of Him — His Spirit.

LB

The county nurse came regularly to take my blood pressure and draw blood for a sedimentation rate, complete blood count, serum protein electrophoreses test and also the rheumatoid factor, which always proved negative. Results were sent to Mayo Clinic through the local hospital laboratory. My doctor would then contact me by telephone, letter or sometimes through my local doctor.

When four weeks had passed, we were able to secure the services of a homemaker through the county nurses' association. She helped with bed baths and light housekeeping for one year. It was good. This is a very worthwhile service. My children continued to help whenever necessary. One of them came the first of the week to change my bed, and the homemaker did it at the end of the week. The laundry was done and we always had clean clothing.

Clarence learned some basics in the kitchen. Sometimes the smells came wafting into the bedroom and I knew what was going on in "my" kitchen. No "burnt offering" ever came in on my tray. The chef did a very good job. I am certain it was more difficult for him than for me at times.

He had some unexpected help from a local restaurant which was owned and operated by good friends of ours. Clarence was remodeling part of their restaurant during these months. They insisted he bring the evening meal home from the restaurant. He didn't object. One daily meal of such very good food was all that was necessary.

Food tasted good to me and surprisingly, I had a good appetite. I needed to lose the excess weight I had gained, but needed the kind of food that would contribute to good health. I was very grateful for the tasty food from the restaurant.

Kind friends, neighbors and relatives brought many tasty dishes and showed their love and concern in many nice ways. Their visits and gifts of love continued faithfully as long as I was bedfast. We were truly blessed. We live in a caring community. It would have been much more difficult if they had not been nearby.

In late June of that first year, our daughter, Judy, and her two little girls moved to our place from Chicago. Star was six years old and Lora was three. We had plenty of room for them and Judy's teenage stepdaughter, Eydie.

We have an old style farm house designed for two families to live under one roof with separate living arrangements. If this old house could talk, it would have many stories to tell — stories of changes that came about because families grew and needs differed throughout the years since its simple log and board walls held one Baer family before this century. In 1900 it became a two-family house and has been since.

It has always been a welcoming house. Friends and strangers felt that caring people lived here. We want to keep it like that. Thre has always been and still is a lot of activity inside our home; births and deaths, sadness and laughter have filled these rooms of happy people with plenty to eat and share in good or lean times.

Judy moved into the smaller apartment in the house. The door between her rooms and ours was often open. She was a real helper in our time of need. She often brought food and we would all eat together in my room. She helped with cleaning, shopping, laundry, gardening and whatever there was to do. Most important and truly appreciated was her help with my personal needs. Her help was a comfort to Clarence and relieved the rest of the family considerably.

Relocating was a strain on Judy and her girls at first, but we enjoyed all of them going in and out. When I read stories for my granddaughters, they held the books and turned the pages. I could neither hold a book nor write at that time. Those were doctor's orders. Not to be able to use my hands was quite hard, because when I talk my hands have a way of wanting to express themselves, too. When I needed rest, the girls would often go to sleep beside me on my bed. Often we played games, simple games like one of us describing an object in the room for the other to guess what the object was. The little girls were always delighted when I could help play. I was surprised at the different games they thought of playing just for my benefit. Isn't love great?

We all tried to live as normally as possible. Clarence drove forty miles each Sunday to teach a Sunday School class, just as we did before I was bedfast. The children attended their respective places of worship. I was not afraid to stay alone and I was happy that they all wanted to attend regularly. I was content and knew the importance to their growing families and to us. Not all of our children had become Christians.

My family treated me royally. They changed beds, emptied chamber pots, swept floors, dusted, prepared food, designed and made a special apparatus to make my bed area convenient and sometimes just sat down to chat.

One of our sons made a "switchboard" for me specially wired for the infra-red lights required for therapy, for the radio and cassette player they gave me for Christmas, for a reading lamp, for a TV and for my hospital bed. He also made the overhead infra-red light frame and wired the telephone to my bedside for emergency use and to keep in touch with friends or relatives. Nothing was physically wrong with my speaking muscles, but because my arm muscles and hands were unable to function well, I managed to lay the receiver on my pillow and turn my head so my ear rested upon it.

I suffered much pain during this first year of confinement.

Pains were so severe that I thought sometimes I could pound the bed or scream. But what good would that have done, except to scare someone (maybe me, too) or draw attention to myself? Some people may find relief in pounding and screaming. For me, when the pains were intense enough for tears, tears came. When it went beyond tears, I found it a good time to reflect on what Jesus had done for me and is still doing for us earth creatures. Another good friend told me he does the same thing when he has seemingly unbearable pain.

It was also a good time for me to sing. Anyone hearing me may have called it something else, but it was at least a painfully joyful noise. Sometimes I sang for a long time and I believe the Lord understood and received glory from it.

God bless good Christian friends and relatives. Times of pain were good times to visit with them. Complaints are not necessary with them. I really did not care to complain or indulge in self pity. That would have been just another pain. I have a high tolerance to pain, but sometimes it did not seem so.

Suffering that we as normal Christian people bear at times is nothing compared to what Jesus suffered when He hung in shame upon the cross. A crucifixion death is horrible. Criminals, especially non-Roman citizens, were often crucified. Jesus, 'guilty' of being the Son of God, but not guilty of blasphemy as He was accused, was crucified as any criminal would have been.

The difference was — Jesus was really there because of me! Have you realized it was for you too? His was the trauma of separation from the Father in order to bear the sins of the whole world. His was a pain that we know nothing about, all because of love and mercy and to bring peace to mankind.

In Matthew 11:28-30 Jesus said, "My yoke is easy and my burden light." When we become partners with Jesus at his invitation we become the other member of a team that is 'hitched' to the yoke. He steadily pulls the half we cannot pull by ourselves, and then pulls some of our load when necessary. He does want us to pull responsibly.

I believe it is easier because of this teamwork to live the life of a Christian than to live a life without Christ. I have experienced it. A Christian who is God's normal person already because he has chosen to be God's child, can live guilt free. He has been restored to freedom, but not to innocence; not freedom to carouse and sin, but freedom to choose not to sin. We can live with the knowledge of sins forgiven, looking hopefully with assurance to an eternal inheritance with Jesus. We have joy, purpose and fulfillment in living. This is what I had.

23

We may have some hard times within this world where we live, but I like to think of them as challenges, a part of normal Christian living. They need not rob us of peace that comes from depending on and walking with God. Galatians 2:20 says, "I have been crucified with Christ and I no longer live, but Christ lives in me. The life I live in the body, I live by faith in the Son of God, who loved me and gave himself for me."

Because I love the Lord, He gave and still gives me real joy in my heart. It is not the kind of joy and happiness of the flesh that makes some people want to jump about and shout. It was and is for me a deep, satisfying, sincere, spiritual joy that gives peace and contentment to my soul and mind. It also gives me a great desire and yearning for others to know and experience His love.

Unbelievers are tortured by guilt and uncertainty of the future. They do not seem to realize that it is fatal and final if not released. They have only hollow, unsatisfied, aimless, selfish, lustful, prideful desires. Let's face it. Sometimes Christians forget and seek after and succumb to these same selfish things. That grieves the Holy Spirit.

It does not mean that we as Christians do not, may not or cannot enjoy and appreciate some things that are in the world. The world is where we live every day and it was made for us to enjoy while living in it. The evil in the world has no hold on the Christian, so his desires are channeled in better directions.

It of course depends on our view of Christ. What kind of commitment do we have? Satan is a defeated foe when we claim Christ as Lord of our lives, and evil temptations and desires fade.

The older a person becomes in his Christian life, the more he can see the futility of yielding to the many seducing evil temptations and desires in the world. Satan does not bother an unbeliever much, except to keep him blinded to the truth. He already has a hold on him. He picks on people who are trying to reveal the truth of God's Word and testify of Jesus. An example from my own life is the best example I can give. I know it for a fact.

Satan blinked at me to see how I would react one day while I was bedfast. Satan did not want me to prepare our Bible Study Group's outline for an in-depth study about Satan and Hell according to the Scriptures. I was preparing to tell how Satan came to be, who he is and about his devious ways.

I felt an extremely hot flush come over me and I could not write one word. I closed my books and started to analyze this strange feeling.

Suddenly I knew! Satan does not like the truth. I believe he was mocking God. I also knew that Satan is a defeated foe, so I calmly opened my books again, laid out my papers and began to write. It took no shouting or command from me because the Lord took care of the situation.

When we resist Satan he flees from us. We cannot afford to be looking for Satan all the time. We dare not make time for him and give him the attention he wants. Jesus is greater, never doubt it for a minute! We need to keep our minds on Christ, not on Satan.

I recalled an experience I had while we were serving in our church hospital in Puerto Rico from 1963-69. I thought of the big difference between the two experiences and how good it is to know that God is everywhere present to keep His children.

Here is a shortened version of what happened.

By request I arranged flowers for the front table of the church while I was in Puerto Rico. In a land where the flowers grow and bloom in abundance, it was a pleasure.

One Easter season I needed something special with a meaningful message for the Good Friday service. I found what I wanted, but a crown of thorns was missing. I went with scissors to the place I remembered a young orange tree grew with thorns.

While cutting the twigs, the thorns scratched and cut my legs and arms. They bled. While I was kneeling in the pathway, fashioning the crown, the stiff sharp thorns tore again at my flesh and the blood dripped on the ground.

I thought of Jesus Christ and found myself singing the song titled "Blessed Redeemer."

Blessed Redeemer

Copyright 1921 in "Songs of Redemption." Renewal 1949 by H. D. Loes
Assigned to John T. Benson, Jr.

AVIS BURGESON CHRISTIANSEN

HARRY DIXON LOES

1. Up Cal-vary's mountain one dreadful morn, Walked Christ my Saviour, weary and worn;
2. "Fa-ther, forgive them!" thus did He pray, E'en while His life-blood flowed fast a-way;
3. O how I love Him, Sav-iour and Friend, How can my prais-es ev - er find end!

Fac-ing for sin-ners death on the cross, That He might save them from endless loss.
Pray-ing for sin-ners while in such woe— No one but Je - sus ev - er loved so.
Thro' years un-num-bered on heaven's shore, My tongue shall praise Him for-ev-er-more.

Chorus

Bless-ed Re-deem - er! pre-cious Re-deem - er! Seems now I
Bless-ed Re-deem-er! bless-ed Re-deem - er!

see Him on Cal-va-ry's tree; Wound-ed and bleed - ing, for sin-ners
Wound-ed and bleed-ing,

plead - ing— Blind and un-heed - - ing— dy-ing for me!
for sin-ners plead-ing— Blind and un-heed - ing—

Used by permission.

The tears flowed freely. I could not stop them nor did I try. Suddenly the Spirit of the Lord touched me with a warmth that bathed me from the top of my head to the tip of my toes. His presence pervaded my whole being to comfort me. I finished the crown, trying it on gently for size, then went to put it in place in the church at the foot of a cross I had shaped of flowers within a mass of flowers.

I had been wrestling with the thought that perhaps I should quit arranging flowers. Maybe it detracted from the sermon, or looked too professional, because people told me they looked forward from one Sunday to the next to see what I would bring. I did not think that seemed quite right. After this thorn experience I had no problem anymore and took care of the table arrangements regularly. People remembered the special arrangement because it spoke to them of Christ.

Some people may say I received the 'baptism of the Holy Spirit' when my body was bathed with warmth. That depends on the definition of the word baptism.

I believe I received the 'baptism of the Holy Spirit' when I took Jesus as Lord and Savior of my life. I believe it is a completed past action because He is given freely to anyone who confesses Him as Lord and accepts His forgiveness for their sins. I believe the Spirit here exercised His divine power in comforting me with peace in my heart. God is faithful and this was Him keeping His promise. It was a very special, holy, spiritual time. The Holy Spirit soothes and calms, the evil spirit disturbs, irritates and never satisfies.

After the first year passed, the inflammation rate was still high. The doctor told me to continue the bedfast treatment and infra-red light therapy. I was not surprised, but I was disappointed. I was not discouraged because I had improved a bit. I enjoyed a friend's description of my progress, "You are making haste slowly."

My leg muscles were less sore and painful and the doctor permitted me now to shower twice weekly. What a relief! I began to flex my leg muscles as soon as I could, for I planned to walk again one day. I exercised my arms with an overhead system of ropes and pulleys Clarence made. Sometimes it was difficult, sometimes impossible. My arms felt best when I positioned the head of my bed up, but my legs said to keep flat without pressure. I did what caused the least discomfort to both. When I remained very still with my arms close to my side, I hardly felt pain, just discomfort. When I moved it proved painful. I could not lie on my side because the pressure increased the pains in my shoulders. A bothersome abdominal hernia also demanded that I stay on my back. I was well cared for and no bedsores developed.

Time passed. As improvement continued, I could do more for myself. In 1982 some young mothers wanted to learn more about the Bible in a study group with me leading. That opportunity I felt I could not pass by. It was a special blessing for them and for me. By sliding books on bed covers and propping them with pillows, I was able to study and write. It took me a long time to prepare, for I needed to put the materials aside often to rest or when the pain worsened. Judy or the girls, who were such willing helpers, put the books I wanted on the bed within reach so I could go at my own very slow pace. I wanted to keep my mind busy and it was wonderful to be able to do this.

At the request of the young mothers we started with book study in Genesis, but the study format was flexible so that we had the freedom to discuss another subject if we needed to.

One evening the question of healing was raised. I began outlines and study to lead the group's discussion. It developed into a piece of writing with facts from the Bible that now has become this book.

Daily I tried to remember that I was God's child created for a purpose. I wanted to use my time wisely. I believe that as long as we live here on earth, God has a purpose for us. Sometimes it may be hard to understand, but I believe it is true. I believe we need to make ourselves available to Him, though, in order to better understand this truth. It takes active faith in Christ Jesus. I believed God allowed me this time in bed for the work He allotted to me.

The Lord and I communicated daily and He, through the Spirit, brought to my remembrance information to write. He guided as I searched for new insights. I believe the Bible teaches that this is the way it should work. I often put the light on at night when I could not sleep and made notes about writing or thoughts to research. I am thankful to God for His directions as I concentrated on this study.

I was also privileged to prepare a special booklet called "A Legacy of Love" for our grandchildren for Christmas, 1982., In all these writing efforts, Judy kindly ran around for me to get paper, type, proofread my big scrawling words and make copies. A sister-in-law willingly typed the first copy of the manuscript for this book on healing. It was not easy to ask for help all the time and it was not always easy for Judy to give it, but she willingly did. She had her own family, but also took repsonsibility when dinner or overnight guests came and to keep the household running smoothly.

Another wonderful thing happened in 1982! For the first time in five years I could stretch! Only my legs from the hips down. And only slightly, but what an event! It was a good sign of improvement. I was so excited, I called the children and other family members and friends. If you have never enjoyed a good invigorating stretch from the top of your head to the tip of your toes, you are missing a real energizer. My arms felt their first stretch much later.

Sometimes people asked, "Don't you get bored?"

I happily told them I had nothing about which to be bored. Two and one-half years sounds like a long time to be bedfast, but for me time passed quickly. With plenty to keep my mind occupied, how could I be bored?

The old maxim "Variety is the spice of life" came to life in my room.

When I was finally able to do more with my hands I began to make birthday cards to send to family, including great-grandnieces and nephews, and friends. The card project almost was too much, but I enjoyed it and wanted to continue it for a full year of birthdays and events. The little girls enjoyed helping me and I devised a system of pillows and propping when necessary.

Therapy took one and one-half hours each morning and each evening. I also had visitors nearly every day.

Scenes through my bedroom windows never ceased to bring me pleasure.

A few days ago I found a copy of some Christmas letters written and sent while I was bedfast. It will show you why I thought my room was not a boring place. Not everything was pain and problem and threadbare carpet. Other important experiences took place in my room and outside my windows. Perhaps it will help some of you to know what possibilities are waiting to be explored or shared with someone else who needs help. Perhaps you stare at city walls.

Here are portions of some letters:

"Take a look with me out through my bedroom windows to the south and east and see what I might see in a day's time as I feast my eyes on the outside world. Each season has its own beauty. I am truly grateful for this big wide wonderful world in which we live.

The other morning we had a light snowfall. As I looked out I thought to myself, 'The trees look especially gray against the pure whiteness.' Even the rail fence looked extra gray against the fall plowed brown earth in the field beyond. As the sun came out and shone in its brilliance and warmth, the snow disappeared and I saw a different picture. In one nook of the rail fence is my summer sitting log that is now unoccupied. It has some green moss on its bark and some of the rails and tree stumps have bits of moss on them, too. Some wood Clarence split for the furnace and fireplace is also ranked there in a nook.

Some plants continue to bravely hold onto their leaves and the lawn grass is still green. The birds seem to be looking for more sheltered places, although sometimes I see a flash of red as a pair of cardinal birds swoop by, with their beady black eyes looking for seeds. Then the flashy blue jays sound their raucous cry as they glide to a position under through the apple tree onto the fence, then hop up to a tree or down on the ground, looking for some goodies. I am sure they will soon discover a newly placed bird feeder hanging from a branch of an apple tree.

Our grandson and his friends from a class at church made and hung it where I could see it. It was a thoughtful thing to do. I enjoyed the pretty birds all spring, summer and autumn and am hoping some will stay all winter.

Then Casey, the cat, takes her daily walk on the top rail of the fence until she pounces on her prey below. Sometimes she misses.

Molly, the dog, makes her daily rounds in the yard. The wild rabbits scamper for cover when Molly appears. One early morning she chased a raccoon up the mulberry tree. The sheep frisk back and forth in the lane that leads from the barn to the pasture field.

Judy's three horses use this lane, too. I like to see them speed sometimes, hooves pounding, heads up and tails flying. Of course, I like horses. Our little spotted calf, Charley, I do not see often. He was led into the yard once so I could see him. He is too young, so he stays in the barn where the chickens are most of the time.

Sometimes the chickens scratch the earth around the trees in the yard or by the fence. We have one rooster with gorgeous golden-orange-rust-red plumage. When the sun shines on him, he almost glows.

Then every now and then Clarence walks by the window, or Judy, or the grandchildren wave to me, some friends walk in to visit and the picture is not gray.

A dear friend surprised me one day with some good binoculars. I could almost bring the outdoors inside with them.

This is just a sample of what I have seen through my windows. Many times we fail to see the whole picture in life and miss some real beauty, earthly and spiritual beauty.

I have also seen and felt the summer sun shine hot and bright. The moon, true to course, shines full and fades again.

The wind, always invisible, fans the tree leaves gently while a mother bird protects her babies on the nest. Or it blows wildly while the tree leaves cling desperately to their roots and clouds bank up stormily as thunder rolls and lightning flashes. Then the rain falls just as wet as usual, and maybe suddenly stops and a rainbow appears. God's remembrance! I remember what an exciting event it was when Lora saw her first rainbow.

Whether it is fair weather and fair health or stormy weather and stormy health, we have so much for which to thank our creator God.

Many other incidents kept me in touch with the outside world through my windows.

Once two cats were fighting so viciously that the fur flew. One cat finally stretched out on the grass and lay there very still with its head partially lifted. The other cat turned and walked slowly away, but it was the obvious victor. All five of our guinea fowl strolled over in front of the cat laying in the grass. They lined themselves up tightly side by side and went through some peculiar motions. While standing still, they stretched out their necks and heads as far as they could and proceeded to move them back and forth in unison about six times, all the while scrutinizing the cat. Then all of them moved around to the other side of the cat and went through the same ritual. Suddenly the cat switched its tail about three times and slowly got up with a bruised looking expression and slunk away to the protection of the rail fence. The curious guineas went about their normal business of pecking the grass. In less than a minute some sparrows flew down from a nearby tree to pick up all the cat fur, leaving the arena clean.

What did it all mean? They were all obedient to the nature God gave them. I never cease to be amazed at the workings of God's vast creation, even through my window.

We have heard complaints that God is far away or does not seem to care. How can this be? Even nature hears and obeys. The seeming silence of God sometimes speaks loudly when we are listening; unrelieved pain, His longsuffering in allowing evil to abound, or maybe a prayer not answered the way we believe it should be or as soon as we think it ought to be. The Christian believer can apply here what Jesus said to the apostle Peter in John 21:22, "What is that to you? You must follow me." Also, "If Jesus learned obedience from what He suffered," (mostly in silence) can we do less? Hebrews 5:8. Obedience is so important for us.

God created us in His image to be special persons. He gave us souls. He made us as people who are to subdue the earth. He gave us power and minds with which to think and reason. We can live by love! Perhaps we reason too much sometimes and forget to feel and love. We place ourselves in the wrong position. We forget to be humble. In the Talmud, a Jewish saying suggests that to keep them humble they must remember that the flea was created first, before man. The creation of people in the image of God ought to be a most humbling and awesome wonder. It takes some heart searching and mind cleansing to keep us in this humble position. It takes right relationships with our fellowmen.

Here is another excerpt from one of our Christmas letters:

"If Jesus came to reconcile and forgive, then we too should do the same for each other." Matthew 6:14, 15 says if we do not forgive each other then Jesus will not forgive us. Have we ever asked each other for forgiveness for anything? Things unknown or known, specifics or nonspecifics, grievous or nongrievous, shady untruths or outright lies, thefts by possessions or reputations, unclean thoughts or actions, deceitfulness, grudges, unkind thoughts or remarks, or evil imaginations?

"We already forgive you and ask that you please take time right now and forgive us. Living here with Christian liberty is a cooperative venture and a great responsibility and privilege. Jesus makes it all possible. Forgiveness, love and peace is the theme for Christmas which we celebrate yearly. We believe that God will bless us abundantly when we try to serve Him obediently wherever we are or whatever we do and in whatever situation we are in."

This is true when we are well or when we are sick.

The second year in bed passed quickly, too. In addition to our Bible studies and the writing I was engrossed in, other good activities brought enjoyment.

Our family likes summer picnics and outdoor functions. They met at their homes sometimes but I heard about the good fun time and they always brought food for me. When they met at our place they planned it for the south and east yards so I could join the fun. The children were thoughtful and included me.

When our two oldest grandsons each got a motorcycle, they drove them into the yard and up to my window so I could see them. When our son fixed up an old tractor, he cranked it up and putt-putted it into the yard right up to my window so I could admire the final coat of bright green paint.

A school science project came into my room. School papers and books were often shared. Kittens came in, new little bunnies, puppies with unopened eyes because the girls couldn't wait any longer to show Grandma. Strange bugs, furry crawly caterpillar worms, pretty leaves or an extra big, juicy, red ripe strawberry, a twig full of lovely yellow apples to hang on the curtain rod, the first tomato of the season, the first bucketful from the potato harvest, a squash or slice of melon all brought the outside in with family love.

Sometimes an ice cream cone came dripping all the way from the ice cream shop two miles away on a summer day! The homemade ice cream was especially good!

We lived normally under special conditions with extra caring touches I appreciated.

Several times a newly stitched quilt was brought for me to see. A new piece of material, a new dress or coat, a recipe to read and share were welcomed guests. Friends often brought handwork like crocheting or embroidery and visited while they worked; or just for me to see. A local Care group met in my bedroom so I could be part of the group. Sometimes they brought supper and spent the evening. A Sunday School class or Bible class, even children's summer Bible school classes shared their sessions with me, sometimes cramped for space in my bedroom. Community churches in addition to my home church were supportive.

The congregation of the church Clarence attended was faithful in keeping in touch with me. They often telephoned, sent audio tapes or scrapbooks, brought dinner and ate with us. Some friends brought guitars to play and sing for me. They sent or brought flowers and plants and came to visit. It was great!

From the time the first tulips bloomed in the spring until frost in the fall, I had fresh flowers in my room. Even the lowly dandelion found its way in. The wild flowers from the woodland and ditch banks, a flowering branch from a tree, or an evergreen sprig for the wintertime graced my room. People from near and far remembered me. How could I feel anything less than special and loved and truly thankful to God? I needed these lovely people and all their gestures of love.

This kind of communication is wonderful. It is marvelous how God gives us this "blood relationship." That is the best term I can give it. We become one through Jesus' blood. It is called love. It is divine love, compassionate love, forgiving love, redeeming love, a kindred love. It is this love from above that gave me real joy and contentment while I was confined. I did not get depressed or feel isolated from family, friends, church and community.

Neither was I isolated or separated from the Lord. I had the assurance that I was bearing fruit and abiding in Christ. I pray that anyone in a similar situation may have this same assurance. The touch from God is wonderful and without contest.

Visitors sometimes asked, "Don't you get very tired and weak?"

I remember a time when I never got tired! I could not say that now, but amazingly enough, I never felt weak. I hurt, but I did not have a weakness like I heard described by people when they had the flu or felt faint. I have never fainted. I felt strong, actually, but I knew with an unused body I should feel weak. I had no strength to lift things, because the pain stopped

35

me, but my body felt strong. Does that make sense? I think it was God's sense.

I often heard, "I know I could not do what you are doing." The Lord did not allow my kind of experience for those persons. He allowed it for me. John 14:15 says, "If you love me you will obey me." Once again, "What is that to you? Follow thou me." That was meant for me.

You may have caught on by now that I enjoy my Christian life! I would not want any other life style. I often sang a song written by William J. Kirkpatrick. The lyrics are:

Singing I go along life's road,
Praising the Lord, Praising the Lord.
Singing I go along life's road,
For Jesus has lifted my load.

It is a good song to sing when you have experienced it. My bedroom was not a dingy attic or prison room. It was a place where love lived. All the caring expressions of love and concern were important in the getting well process.

Even the persons who came and told me that perhaps I had unconfessed sin or not enough faith for healing, soon sensed that faith and love lived in my room. It was good to visit with them. They wanted to help. It was their right and not a time for me to argue or panic.

It is good to remember that just because a person seems to be out of circulation by being bedfast or housebound or is handicapped, he or she is not incapable of thinking or making decisions. Do not ignore that person. He need not be robbed of dignity and made to feel worthless, unwanted or isolated. It is good to let him know what goes on in the family, church and community, whether it is good or bad news. Let him decide what to do with it. Many prayers can ascend to God from a limited position! Low whispered voices and remarks are not healthy. I heard little of this. Perhaps in some extreme cases, depending on the temperament of the confined person, it may be necessary to withhold some news at certain times. Ordinarily not. When a person can think but has no chance to exercise the mind by communicating with family and friends, his mind will probably soon begin to fade and finally become blank. That is a sad situation. I did not want that to happen to me.

I was so thankful I could be in my own home. Not everyone is that privileged. I can understand through experience that a person in a limited position would be vulnerable to all kinds of propaganda and beliefs that offer false hope. It could be a confusing time. It is important to be firmly grounded in the Word of God. We must read and pray often. It is what makes us grow and keeps us healthy spiritually; also physically.

Medication, especially over medication, sometimes does strange things to the mind and body. There may have been times when the family thought I was not thinking properly. They may have thought I was joining the ranks of senior citizens who are allowed to act strangely! I may instead have had my head in the clouds trying hard to remember some thought I wanted to write on paper as soon as I could reach the paper. I do believe a person in a limited situation needs to work harder to keep a healthy mind. Even with a healthy mind, it is a task to keep one. I tried. It is best not to depend totally on the help of others when possible, but to accept help graciously when necessary. It is wonderful to accept help from the Lord.

I had good news in March of 1983. For the first time, my sedimentation rate was down to 50. In June it went down to 47. I was encouraged. In July, however, severe pains attacked me again. We arranged for a reevaluation at Mayo Clinic. With me on a stretcher in the back of a van, Clarence and Judy took turns driving for the twelve-hour journey from Ohio to Minnesota. We drove during the night to avoid heavy traffic and heat, and arrived at 6 a.m. when the day's activity at the clinic was beginning.

My former doctor had retired, so another kind doctor scheduled the required tests. He reported what the tests showed, "You have many inflammations and the cartilage in your knee joints is gone."

We discussed the possibility of putting in new artificial joints. I had not even thought about that possibility before. Now, what shall we do?

My abdominal hernia was such a lump that I did not think I could learn to walk again on new knees until it was taken care of properly. The doctors then examined me abdominally. The x-rays did not show everything I felt inside my body. I told them how I felt and how it seemed to be, although I could not see inside my body. They said they would operate if I really decided it was necessary, but they rather believed the knees were more important. They made it my choice.

I said, "The abdomen must be taken care of first." As long as I took prednisone, my local doctor would not consider abdominal surgery. The hernia became increasingly worse during that time and even worse during my bedfast years. It began to cause elimination problems and discomfort I understood even if the X-rays showed no major problems.

We waited days at Mayo for a surgery date.

Clarence and Judy were in and out of my room often, but because I was out so much for tests and preparation, they had a chance in twelve days to see Rochester. We still had no definite date, but Judy needed to go home to her little girls who stayed with our son, his wife and four boys.

The day after she left, the report was given to us that surgery would be the following Monday, if my decision was still the same.

The doctors were surprised when on August 8 they performed a three-hour surgery. They agreed I had made a wise decision. I was very sick for several days. We prayed for strength. When on the twelfth day the doctor said I could make plans to go home, I was willing.

Judy and her girls, and our oldest son came to get Clarence and me. I had been at Mayo for four weeks, and even though I was suffering the same joint and muscle problems as before plus the tender abdominal incision, I was willing to go home to recover. If I had known what lay ahead on that trip home, I may have reconsidered!

We battled miles and miles of road repairs. Again, we traveled at night to avoid heat and heavy traffic. The inescapable jostling and bumping was almost too much for my new incision. In Madison, Wisconsin, we stopped to get an air flight home. There was none until the following day, so we drove on. We arrived safely at home after a twenty-hour hectic trip. It was such a relief to be home. The family was waiting for us in the front yard with a picnic prepared for our homecoming.

During my recovery period at home I was advised to begin using a wheel chair and also to do some walking to prepare for knee surgery later. My leg bones had become slightly soft from medication and being little used, my trusty cane helped me greatly. My general condition began to improve nicely after the abdominal surgery.

In November I reported to Mayo again. This time for knee joint replacements.

Nurses came to my room, looked me over and repeatedly said, "You are brave for having both knees done at one time." I was not certain if they thought I was brave or if they just wanted to cheer me. I could not say if I was brave or not because I had never had this done before. I am sure the doctors would not have allowed it if they thought I could not handle it. They knew me inside-out and upside-down by this time. I think if I needed to have it done again, I would do both at the same time. It was interesting to learn that one of their staff doctors had the same surgery on one knee and said he did not know anything could hurt so much. He had performed knee surgery on other people; now it was his turn!

I had my first experience with male nurses taking care of me. They gave me good care! I felt sorry for one young student nurse. I was his first solo bed bath patient. When I was ready to leave the hospital, he came in especially to thank me for making it easy for him.

What a testimony we can give in such circumstances! Our attitudes, conduct and appreciation speak loudly at such times. One young nurse asked, "is this what you call a Bible?" she picked it up from my bedside table as if she considered it a special privilege to touch it. We sometimes forget just how special it is.

It seems as if I was given special opportunities to witness to the power of God whenever and wherever I was hospitalized. One time when I was hospitalized at another clinic, a 27-year-old woman was moved into my room. During the evening her brother and father came to see her, bringing news that another brother was killed in a highway accident. She, of course, was shocked, began to scream and cry. Nothing seemed to quiet her.

I was already in bed and ready for lights out, because that morning I had surgery on my head to test for inflammation in the veins. My head was wrapped up like a mummy. I could see, so I carefully got out of bed and went to her bedside. I held her hand and asked her and her family if I could pray with them. They consented.

Great calmness came upon them all. When I finished, I went back to my bed.

Her father and brother thanked me many times for what I did. Praise the Lord when we can testify for Him when we are sick or well!

Then we ask, "For such a time as this . . . am I here?" I received so many lovely cards and letters in the hospital building where I had abdominal surgery and in the building for knee surgery. Receiving cards was a testimony to a loving God, and caring friends many miles away. It impressed the doctors and nurses. One of my roommates seemed to know little about Christianity. She enjoyed looking at my cards. Her one and only card was obscene.

When the day came for me to be released from the hospital I could travel by car. Clarence and I headed for home in zero degree temperatures. We had car trouble a few hours after leaving Mayo. I waited in the car, bundled in blankets, while Clarence walked for help. Some helpful young people stopped. Instead of taking money for their help, they said, "Pass it on!" It reminded me of the good Samaritan of the Bible.

I was glad to get home after twenty-two days away. We missed Thanksgiving at home, but enjoyed Christmas especially, because it was at home with our family.

Clarence did more city footwork that year than ever before in his life. He spent weeks away from home for me. Thank God for good husbands. At Mayo we met some people whose family could not stay with them. Although it worked out well for them, I was glad Clarence was able to be with me.

I used crutches for several months. That was difficult for my arms and hands, but good for my legs and new knee joints. After the crutches, I used a cane until September of 1984. Since then I only use it occasionally, as a person uses aspirin for a headache. It is not a habit, just a very good help.

I have had checkups since the surgery and all seems well. My legs were straightened by using a cast on one and the other was automatically bent and exercised by a machine. When the cast came off, the machine was attached to that leg. It was painful. Now I can walk with both legs. The use of my arms and hands is limited, but both are much better than when I went to bed in 1981.

Now that I am well and seeing people publicly again, they tell me that they never expected to see me out of bed and walking! The Lord has blessed in a marvelous way. I never gave up hope. I never felt that God would not do for me what He thought best for me and for those around me.

Was this a miracle?

It is a miracle in that a miracle is an event that transcends the laws of nature. When Jesus performed miracles He confirmed His Deity and God's redemptive powers for the souls of people. He said by His presence that the promised Messiah had come. By faith we believe this and, because we believe, He, time and time again, proves His faithfulness to His children by the care He extends to them. This is His mercy, an extension of His grace.

I believe it is most important to remember that the Lord is faithful and His promises are true and believable. Along with God's faithfulness is our faithfulness to Him and His Word.

My faith has not wavered and the time spent in confinement was not wasted. My faith only grew stronger because of God's faithfulness. It was a time of faith confirmation and faith stretching.

I believe the Lord faithfully gives His children blessings for being obedient and faithful, and it is not termed a miracle. It is normal for God to do this. I believe the word 'miracle' is often used carelessly, and probably misused as often as is the word 'love.' God made a world with people in it and did not stop at that point in caring for it. He wants to share with us in love. Salvation itself is a love miracle. Can you think what it would be like without this miracle?

If my recovery seems like a miracle to you — Praise and thank God!

If it seems like a special blessing because of faithfulness — Praise and thank God!

If someone is helped by reading this — Praise and thank God!

I know the Lord has in a wonderful way administered the whole process during this period of time. I do not know what the future will bring. What I do not totally understand I accept by faith and trust His judgment. It is by the Lord's mercies, the help of doctors, nurses, hospitals, relatives, friends and a dear loving family that I can say as it says in Psalm 34:3, "Oh, magnify the Lord with me, and let us exalt His name together."

May the Lord be pleased to add His blessing.

He Counted Us Worthy

God counted us worthy from heaven above
Worthy on earth to pour out His love
Worthy on earth to receive of His Spirit
Worthy on earth our guilt to acquit.
God counted us worthy when we'd fallen from grace
He counted us worthy to restore us a place.
He counted us worthy, our Savior Divine
He counted us worthy to use of His time.
He counted us worthy to tell His good news
Salvation is free, there is no excuse.
God counted us worthy from heaven above,
Worthy on earth to receive of His love.
How can we not humbly accept His great plans
Trusting His wisdom far greater than man's.
God counted us worthy, just why we know not,
Except that He made us and we each have a spot.
He counted us worthy we truly believe,
Created us persons, His love to receive.

L.B.

PRAISE TO THE LORD, THE ALMIGHTY

LOBE DEN HERREN 14 14 4 7 8

Joachim Neander, 1680
Lobe den Herren, den mächtigen König der Ehren
Tr. Catherine Winkworth, 1863

Gesangbuch, Stralsund, 1665

1 Praise to the Lord! the Al-might-y, the King of cre - a - tion!
2 Praise to the Lord! who o'er all things so won-drous-ly reign - eth,
3 Praise to the Lord! who doth pros-per thy work and de - fend thee;
4 Praise to the Lord! O let all that is in me a - dore Him!

O my soul, praise Him, for He is thy health and sal - va - tion!
Shel-ters thee un - der His wings, yea, so gen-tly sus - tain - eth;
Sure - ly His good - ness and mer - cy here dai - ly at - tend thee;
All that hath life and breath, come now with prais-es be - fore Him!

All ye who hear, Now to His tem - ple draw near,
Hast thou not seen How thy de - sires have been
Pon - der a - new What the Al - might - y can do,
Let the A - men Sound from His peo - ple a - gain,

Join me in glad a - do - ra - tion!
Grant - ed in what He or - dain - eth?
If with His love He be - friend thee!
Glad - ly for aye we a - dore Him! A - men.

Books are the carriers of civilization.
Without books history is silent,
literature dumb, science crippled,
thought and speculation at a standstill.

Barbara W. Tuckman
Author and Historian
died in 1989

PART II
Pain, Suffering And Healing: What Does The Bible Say?

Preface

Many books have been written on the subject of illness and healing. Some ideas seem far apart. It causes many different confusing thoughts and voices. I do not wish to add to them. I pray that the Biblical teaching and examples given will help bring about a calm assurance and understanding instead of confusion. We need the whole picture to understand divine healing, not just 'sick verses' picked out here and there. We need the whole scriptures which help establish us in faith and truth.

This is not a book on theology. It is not one of prejudice, fairness or unfairness. This book is written and given to you with the purpose of making understandable the principles of God's love and care for his children. Also, to know the trust we can have in One who so graciously and patiently reigns over us when we are well or ill. I pray that as you read this book you will receive knowledge of the truth.

The subjects are discussed in separate chapters for easy thought and reference. The words used are plain and simple so anyone can read and be informed, edified and encouraged. We often hear remarks like, "I was reading, but I quit. I couldn't understand it. It had too many big words in it." Hopefully it will not be so with this writing. Without an understanding how can knowledge be gained?

Every person has a need to know something and someone.

Every person has a need to belong to someone somewhere.

Every person has a need to believe someone.

Every person has a need to love someone and be loved by someone.

Every person has a need to try to understand that adversity has a place within the Christian vision of the world. It is part of the mysterious dealings of God with people. The Christian is not exempt from the conflicts of life.

In John 11:1-44 we read about the sickness, death and burial of a close friend of Jesus. His name was Lazarus and they knew each other well. Lazarus got sick and the Bible says it was important for him to be sick, to die and be buried. Jesus was glad so that the Father could be glorified. The part about glorifying God is so often forgotten by us earth creatures.

Sickness and other hardships should be remembered as part of life. They are, of course, disruptions. They are on a collision course with health, our particular routine of living, and often with wealth. But what is healthy? Obviously something good. A desirable condition. What is sickness. Obviously something to be gotten rid of. Something undesirable.

Some get-well cards really seem to say, "If you are sick you cannot have happiness. If you are sick you are 'out of it.' Sickness is a shame and it is out of place. Hide it."

Even when someone asks, "How are you?" we often answer, "Fine." when we are not fine. We do not need to give a whole medical history, but we should be honest. We could say, "I have a slight _____. Pray for me." If we are fine, then say so and offer thanks.

It is all part of the total healing and restoration plan for God's people. It would be much better to accept God's dealings with people as part of the glory Jesus wants to give the Father. And how does a person fit in His plan?

Do not quit sending cards when there is a need because it really is helpful and appreciated by those who receive them. To know that you are being remembered is a stimulation and comfort. It encourages a right attitude. Be thoughtful in your choice of card or note.

To heal is to make something better than it is. Sometimes a thing is healed but not cured. Sometimes it is healed and cured. Both imply wholeness. Figuratively speaking, the meaning is similar. Curing seems to include a restoration after a process or action. In this context I am using both words which to me seems right.

For example, our pioneer forefathers prepared meat for future use by putting it in a salt brine, then dripping it and

50

sometimes smoking it. This is curing. In our present day, the injection method is used in the butcher shop. It is also called curing. The meat must be cured just right or it will spoil and be wasted.

One Biblical example of curing for people is David's experience. In Samuel 1 and 2 in the Old Testament, we read much about David. It says he was "a man after his (God's) own heart." 1 Samuel 13:14 and Acts 13:22. God did not want David to have a wasted life, but David sinned. When he repented, he was forgiven, but he was not cured. The curing process went on and David remembered.

Psalm 32 and 51 are results of his bitter experience. Both are good examples of David's written praise to God after repentance and the experience of forgiveness. His sin was gone. He could live guilt free, but the preservation continued.

David's experience will be discussed further in later chapters.

When any one of us receives salvation, our healing is accomplished. "By His stripes or wounds we are healed," Isaiah 53:5. God wants to keep or preserve us, so the curing goes on until the resurrection of the redeemed when we have been restored "holy and unblameable and unreproveable in His sight." Colossians 1:22. (King James Version) The New International Version says, "But now he has reconciled you by Christ's physical body through death to present you holy in His sight, without blemish and free from accusation."

This study on healing includes a look at faith, prayer, the Holy Spirit and the will of God. These are the necessary parts of divine healing. It also includes the book of Job, which is a study on the problem of pain and suffering, as is the suffering of Christ Jesus, Paul and the other apostles, with a continuing Christian heritage.

By the listing of examples and the studying of the background of healing, the purpose is to have a scriptural understanding of an important subject.

Healing is a controversial subject for many people in today's busy world. Is it needed or is it not?

A quick answer could be — the church should teach and practice healing. Or we could repeat an old, old phrase and say, "The Bible says it! I believe it! And that settles it!"

However, so that we know WHY we believe what we believe without any doubting, we will look into the Word and learn what the Lord says is the truth. We will approach this subject from the source and use Biblical examples of suffering and sickness to see how God dealt with different conditions.

I hope this writing will encourage reading the scriptures for learning the truth.

L.B.

God's created world
  expands for humankind.

Chapter I
God Created Man Holy

When God created man, He made him in the image of Himself, a reflection of Himself, God.

Man was holy and had no fear. He was a whole person mentally, physically, emotionally and spiritually. He was in a state of pure love and knowledge that we do not know. Man was in a state of sinlessness without knowing the difference between right and wrong, good and evil — a state of innocence only.

He had pure love, innocence and obedience. He was God conscious and totally dependent on God. He had complete trust in God. He was created to live in a state of communication and harmony with God and nature. He was a specially planned creation.

As for the things of nature, God only spoke the word and they materialized from nothing. Awesome!

With man, God chose to involve some other method, making him from the dust already in place. "God breathed into man the breath of life and man became a living soul." Genesis 2:7. We have been inbreathed by God himself. Again, awesome!

Man was made in the "likeness of us," implying a Father, Son, Spirit image. Genesis 1:26. Ephesians 4:24 says, "Created to be like God in true righteousness and holiness."

The created man was Adam. From him God formed Eve, a woman. Both were created as adults. Together they became the world's first man and wife team. Genesis 1:26, 27 and 2:21-25.

They received a special blessing, that of living in the beautiful and specially created Garden of Eden. How long they lived there we do not know. In Genesis 5:5 we read that Adam died at the age of 930 years. This is the time of his life that we can know about from the Bible.

While Adam and Eve lived in the Garden of Eden where God put them, they had only one known limitation. God forbade them to eat fruit from the tree in the middle of the garden. We do not know what kind of fruit grew on that tree. It was called "the tree of the knowledge of good and evil." Genesis 2:9.

God told them that if they ate of that fruit, they would "surely die." Genesis 2:17. Adam and Eve did not question this.

Together they remained innocent, sinless, wise and righteous, confirming their holiness unto God until they chose to question His command about limitations and listened to Satan who appeared on the scene. Genesis 3:1-6.

Satan is the biggest tragedy of the world. He was once a beautiful angel in heaven. Isaiah 12:12-14, Revelation 12:7-9. Because he became proud and rebelled against God, he could live there no longer. He is powerful, deceitful and persuasive.

He tempted Eve with disobedience and she ate fruit from the forbidden tree. She in turn gave Adam some and he also ate some fruit.

Satan lied and practiced deceitfulness.

Did it happen all at once or very subtly over a period of time? The Bible does not say. It does not say the exact time when Satan was cast out of heaven. Isaiah 12:12-14; Revelation 12:7-9.

The truth is, they did not resist him when he tempted them. They exercised free choice and rejected the grace of God. In verse 6 we read they succumbed to the following:

1. The lust of the flesh — it satisfied appetites.
2. The lust of the eyes — it looked good and created desire.
3. The pride of life — it made one wise and knowledgeable.

They disobeyed God's command. Genesis 2:15-17. At that point they became:

1. Affected spiritually — they became separated from holiness.
2. Affected mentally — they questioned God and willed to disobey.

3. Affected emotionally — it brought fear, shame and guilt for disobedience.

4. Affected physically — they were forced to relocate, labor and sorrow came, also pain at childbirth.

They were banished from the garden. They became infected with sin-sickness and were subject to death.

This is called 'original sin' and is still in effect. This is a fact! In James 1:13, 15, the New International translation says, "When tempted, no one should say, God is tempting me. For God cannot be tempted by evil, nor does he tempt anyone, but each one is tempted when, by his own evil desire, he is dragged away and enticed. Then, after desire has conceived, it gives birth to sin, and sin, when it is full grown, gives birth to death."

Step by step it drags us to death. It was true for Adam and Eve and continues to this day. It will continue until Satan, who has already been judged, will receive his penalty and "Death will be swallowed up in victory." 1 Corinthians 15:54.

When the first man and woman left the garden, they became the first parents of the human race. This sick, sin nature and the result of sin — death — was transmitted to their offspring. It was transmitted to the whole race of mankind.

Children born were now born in man's own fallen image. Romans 5:12 says, "Therefore, just as sin entered the world through one man, and death through sin, and in this way death came to all men, because all sinned." Romans 6:23 says, "For the wages of sin is death; but the gift of God is eternal life through Jesus Christ, our Lord."

The wages of love is eternal life. Eternal life is wholeness in Christ. This wholeness of body and soul is what God is interested in for every human being on this earth. Let us take a closer look.

Man's first sin separated man from God. The second sin involved their children, Cain and Abel. It separated man from man. Jesus Christ came to restore both of these relationships. By his sacrifice on the cross and resurrection and ascension, he can restore both. This is what pleases the Father in heaven.

56

Man started to regress when sin arrived. Equality was lost; death, sorrows, pains, suffering began. The ground was cursed or afflicted so that it grew thorns and thistles; they were the enemies of man then and they still are. Man became a slave or prisoner to sin, decay and death. These are Satan's works. Man was sick. The whole body needed healing.

The curing process began when they left the garden.

God placed people on this earth in such a way that they can communicate and have close relationships with each other. They were created to live.

Good people and bad-acting people receive sun and shade together, receive storms and gentle breezes together, receive cold and heat, snow and rain. The very air people share is for the just and the unjust.

All are blessings from God, for the saint and the sinner. This is the physical aspect of living.

The laws of nature are divine. When the laws are misused, people suffer. It affects the mental, emotional and spiritual state of humans.

They respect God for His continual care and control of everything and themselves; or they disregard Him and want control over themselves and all they can touch.

An example in Acts 17 describes Paul, an apostle of Jesus Christ, proclaiming Christ in Athens.

The people were partly ignorant, but they wanted control of their world by serving idols who could not object, talk back or correct them in their selfish pursuits.

Paul observed that the city was full of idols and therefore, the people must be very religious. He refers to the idols as objects of worship in verse 25. If the Athenians believed in existing gods and had idols of them as objects of worship, it was not what God wanted.

Paul enlightened them by telling them the truth. He found one altar to an unknown god and used that as a clue to preach of Jesus Christ to them.

In Verse 24 Paul says, "The God who made the world and everything in it is the Lord of heaven and earth and does not live in temples built by hands. And He is not served by human hands, as if He needed anything, because He himself gives all men life and breath and everything else. From one man He made every nation of men that they should inhabit the whole earth and he determined the times set for them and the exact places where they should live. God did this so that men would seek him and perhaps reach out for Him and find Him, though He is not far from each one of us. For in Him we live and move and have our being. We are His offspring.''

We surely have a God not made by man's design and skill.

Paul spoke to people who had an imbalance in thought and practice. They needed spiritual healing and perhaps a long curing process.

The mind and heart are so created that they seek for something greater than they know most of the time. They long for something which brings some pleasure, contentment and wholeness.

In the search, we are prone to make idols out of things by attaching too much value on certain things and not enough on others. We cause an imbalance.

So it is with the matter of healing the sick. There can be an imbalance in our view of the gifts of the Holy Spirit.

When the Holy Spirit gives gifts, he gives many gifts. He gives them as he wills, but only to a person converted to Christ. 1 Corinthians 12:4 says, "There are different kinds of gifts, but the same Spirit. There are different kinds of service, but the same Lord. There are different kinds of working, but the same God works all of them in all men. Now to each one the manifestation of the Spirit is given for the common good.

"To one there is given through the Spirit the message of wisdom, to another the message of knowledge by means of the same Spirit, to another faith by the same Spirit, to another gifts of healing by that one Spirit, to another miraculous powers, to another prophecy, to another the ability to distinguish between spirits, to another the ability to speak in different kinds of tongues, and to still another the interpretation of tongues. All these are the work of one and the same Spirit, and He gives them to each man just as He determines.''

This is the Word of God and no one should want to deny the Word and the workings of the Spirit.

Ephesians 4 says the gifts are designed to help bring about unity in the church of Jesus Christ. They should also bring growth.

We need to recognize the different gifts in other people and in ourselves. We need to be just as happy for other's gifts if they have one of those listed or if they have other good gifts, as if it were ourselves. The Spirit may give other good gifts "Just as He determines."

That is the only way the Spirit can work freely.

In 1 Corinthians 12:28 the Word says, "And in the church God has appointed first of all apostles, second prophets, third teachers, then workers of miracles, also those having gifts of healing, those able to help others, those with gifts of administration, and those speaking in different kinds of tongues."

Does anyone have all these gifts?

Verse 31 says, "But eagerly desire the greater gifts" and "I will speak of the most excellent way — Love!" If love is not present, the gifts have no value.

Healing is one of these gifts, but it is not emphasized more than any other one. We need to be careful not to deify or make a god out of perfect health. We must not demand or insist that God give it above all else. We need to care for our bodies, this is true; but the Holy Spirit lives in the heart of every consecrated believer in the Lord Jesus Christ when he is well or when he is sick.

The healing of a sin-sick soul is often emphasized throughout the Holy Scriptures. God wants His children to be "Conformed unto the image of His Son." Romans 8:29.

The highest will for man is Christ-likeness and to bring glory to God. This is spiritual.

Jesus says, "They that are whole have no need of a physician, but they that are sick; I came not to call the righteous but sinners to repentance." Matthew 9:12, 13; Luke 5:31, 32 and Mark 2:17, King James Version.

This speaks of the natural to give understanding to the spiritual. It says:

1. There are well people.
2. There are sick people and they need a doctor.
3. There are righteous people.
4. Sinners need to repent.
5. Righteous people have already accepted Christ's call, repented and are healed (made whole spiritually).

This, Jesus says, is most important and the reason why He came.

Healing of the sick and suffering has been done for ages already, but always as God sees best.

Let us look at some examples of God's working with people in the next chapters.

Chapter II
Examples From
The Old Testament

The Old Testament provides many examples of when God's people were healed or not healed.

By listing each example with its specific reference, you will have an easy to read brief description. Then you can also find the complete reference in your own Old Testament for better understanding.

1. Beginning in Genesis we read that Adam and Eve were sent from the Garden of Eden because of their sin of disobedience. In time the earth became populated with people. This was now normal. With the increase in numbers came an increase in evil. Man had become very wicked. Genesis 6:5, 6, 7, says, "Every inclination of the thoughts of His people's heart was only evil all the time. It grieved the Lord that He had made man on the earth and His heart was filled with pain." He had to destroy His creation.

However, healing was extended only to righteous Noah and his family. This is the account of the great flood and a story of God's mercy and justice. Genesis 6-8.

2. In Genesis 27:1 and 35:28, 29 we read about Isaac's blindness because of age. Isaac remained blind until he died.

3. Genesis 35 says Rachel died in childbirth.

4. In Exodus the sicknesses and sufferings of the Israelite people were great. The only healing for them was in God, away from idols and all kinds of magic and evil practices.

5. In Exodus 15:26 is a scripture often quoted and used out of context. It says, "I am the Lord who heals you."

In context we discover that the children of Israel had just crossed the Red Sea in a miraculous way and had traveled three days without water. When they did find some water, it was bitter. The Lord performed a miracle on their behalf after Moses cried out to Him.

The Lord showed Moses a piece of wood. He threw it into the water. The water became sweet.

Then God tested the Israelites and made a decree and a law for them. He said, "If you listen carefully to the voice of the Lord your God and do what is right in His eyes, if you pay attention to His commands and keep all His decrees, I will not bring on you any of the diseases I brought on the Egyptians, for I am the Lord who heals you."

The law at Mount Sinai was not yet given. These were immediate laws. God was trying to impress upon them that He alone was God, that He was holy, that their trust should be in the living God their Savior and rescuer from the hands of the Egyptians and their idolatrous worship.

By trusting and obeying these immediate commands, they would find healing and wholeness.

The natural way for these people would have been that, because of their close association with the Egyptians, they would have carried with them the same diseases. But God would do the unnatural thing by not giving them the diseases if they obeyed Him, demonstrating power and holiness.

6. In Exodus 23, 25 and 26 and Deuteronomy 7:6-15 are verses also often quoted and used out of context. "I will take sickness away from the midst of you and give you a full life span."

Evidently some were sick. God told this to the Israelite people, instructing them about going into the land of Canaan "to possess it."

Reading the entire chapter is important to understanding God's intention.

Not inflicting them was just one of many things that were given to them to test their obedience. The chapter lists many blessings of love for obedience. Their orders were to destroy as they went all objects of idolatry and idols and not "bow down to them."

Again, this was a demonstration of His power and holiness for a particular situation.

In Leviticus, God gave many laws for the physical and spiritual welfare and health of His people. We do well to read them to understand how God is interested in calling a people to be holy.

7. Exodus 4:6, 7 describes how Moses' hand became leprous and then restored so they would believe that the Lord appeared to him.

In Numbers 12 we see Miriam struck leprous and shut out of camp for seven days in shame for sinning. It seems as if jealousy was exercised. Moses prayed and God healed her. She died enroute to the promised land when she was about 130 years old.

8. 1 Samuel 31 says Saul and others committed suicide. What kind of sickness causes people to do this? Pride and selfishness.

9. 2 Samuel 4:4 and 9 speaks of Jonathan's lame son who was not healed.

10. 2 Samuel 11, 12 allows us to examine a part of David's life.

David was a handsome young man with a ruddy complexion according to 1 Samuel 16:12. He was annointed king when he was just a young man.

David committed adultery, planned the murder of the woman's husband and had a child through this adulterous relationship. The child became sick for seven days. In David's grief, he said, "Who can tell whether God will be gracious to me, that the child will live." So he prayed and fasted and was prostrate with grief all the nights, but the child died because of David's sin.

When David said he had sinned and repented, God forgave the sin; but God's promise to David in verse 10 was, "The sword will never depart from your house because you despised me and were adulterous."

God said He would bring calamities upon David — and He did. This was a curing process.

Acts 13:22 leaves no doubt that God allowed this "to fulfill all my will." God speaks plainly.

11. In 1 Kings 13:1-6 we witness that Jeroboam's hand withered and was restored.

12. In 1 Kings 14:1 is the account of Abijah, son of Jeroboam, who became sick. God spoke through the prophet Ahijah to say "he shall die" in verse 12 and in verse 17 he died. This was judgment because Jeroboam did evil and caused Israel to sin.

13. In 1 Kings 17:17 it says Elijah, a prophet of God, restored a child that had fallen very sick and died. He used prayer and touch to restore the child.

14. 2 Kings 4 says Elisha restored a young man who had been sick and died. He also used prayer and touch.

15. In 2 Kings 5 Naaman was cured of leprosy. Jesus said in Luke 4:27, "There were many in Israel with leprosy in the time of Elisha the prophet, yet not one of them was cleansed, only Naaman, the Syrian." Elisha gave the word and Naaman obeyed by washing seven times in the Jordan River. River baths for healing were common in those days. Leprosy was consided emblematic of sin because only God could cure it. Lepers were not commonly allowed in public to wash where others washed. Here, using the natural way typified the spiritual.

16. In the same story, in verse 27, we find Gehazi, the servant, received Naaman's leprosy and it would also cling to his descendants. This was Gehazi's punishment for disobedience.

17. 2 Kings 13:14 describes Elisha as a great man of God. However, he fell sick and died of his sickness. This was physical and he was not healed.

The power of God was once demonstrated in an unusual way here in verses 20, 21. It tells of a man who was hastily thrown into the tomb of Elisha. When the body touched the bones of Elisha the man came to life and stood up on his feet.

How can we possibly understand the power of God? Awesome!

18. 2 Kings 15:5 says the Lord afflicted King Azariah (Uzziah) with leprosy until he died. He was not cleansed or cured.

19. 2 Kings 20:1-11 says King Hezekiah was sick unto death. He prayed and wept. God did the following four things for Hezekiah:

a. God lengthened his life 15 years. This was God's mercy.

b. He moved time back 15 degrees on the sun dial, an unnatural act affecting the community. It was a sign that God would do as He had said — heal him.

c. He ordered a poultice of figs to heal a boil. He used medicine.

d. He commanded that Hezekiah go to church in three days to worship. Hezekiah was healed.

Later on Hezekiah became too proud of his accomplishment in the land. He had acquired much wealth and did not use good judgment concerning it, so the Lord brought punishment to the land. Hezekiah repented and the Lord withheld punishment until after Hezekiah died. This shows a merciful, sovereign Lord.

20. People of Ashdod, Ekron, Gath, Askelon and Gaza were afflicted with tumors for misusing the Ark of God in 1 Samuel: 5, 6.

21. In 2 Kings 6 the Aramaeans were struck with blindness. Some had their eyes opened.

22. 2 Chronicles 16:11-14 tells about King Asa of Judah, a good king, who was diseased in his feet and doctored only with physicians. "He did not seek the Lord at all" and died that way.

23. 2 Chronciles 21:12-20 says Jehoram, king of Judah was stricken with an incurable bowel disease because he did not walk with God and caused others to sin. The Word says his disease was incurable or was so bad that his bowels fell out. Verse 20 says "He died without being desired." How sad. He was not healed.

In the above examples some people were healed, some not. Some reveled in sin, some obeyed God. Some were judged, some punished. Some believed, some did not. Some were stricken with various pains and sufferings through sickness.

In all these examples it is evident that God was very much in power, revealing Himself through mercy and justice.

He revealed Himself as a holy and sovereign God, preserving a godly line of ancestry for the Son of Man, that through Him all nations of the earth are now blessed.

To read about suffering extreme adversity look in Ezekiel 4. Ezekiel lay on his left side for 390 days and on his right side for 40 days as a symbol of what the Jews would experience during the siege of Jerusalem. The food he was commanded to eat would be undesirable by today's standards.

Jeremiah was put in stocks, (Jeremiah 20). Daniel remained faithful in a den of lions, (Daniel 6). Daniel 4:28-37 tells about the unique experience of an unbeliever named Nebuchdnezzar but who later praised God.

Sarah had no sickness but an affliction to be childless. When Sarah was of an old age and her husband, Abraham, 100 years old the Lord blessed them with a son they named Isaac, (Genesis 15-21). Abraham loved Isaac but would have in obedience to God, killed his own son if God had not intervened. 1 Samuel tells about Hannah who was afflicted to be childless. She had bitterness of soul and wept much. By prayer and faithfulness to God she was healed and bore a son Samuel. She in turn gave Samuel back to God for his service. Her thanks and praise are recorded in 1 Samuel . Verse 2 says, "There is no one Holy like the Lord: there is no one besides you; there is no Rock like our God."

Jacob limped because his hip socket was wrenched. Hosea's pain came because of an adulterous wife.

More examples may be found perhaps. Some are more familiar than others. God was always moving to refine a people for His glory and to demonstrate love.

Blessed is the man
who perseveres
under trial,

because when he has
stood the test,
he will receive the
crown of life that
God has promised to
those who love Him.

James 1:12

Chapter III
Job: The Problem Of Pain And Suffering

An outline form of study is used in this chapter.

It begins with a brief outline of the Book of Job, chronologically referenced from chapter one.

After the brief outline to describe the book, an informal outline with comments allows us to look at the author, the many characters interacting with Job and a detailed account of his pain and suffering.

As in earlier chapters, specific references are listed with comments so we can learn of Job's intense experience by reading this study and the Bible together.

In studying the book of Job we could branch off into many different areas. The discussions would be endless.

This study will keep in mind the theme of this book as a whole, The Problem of Pain and Suffering. Let this be the overriding thought as it is read. Reading Job is necessary. Read it individually or have a group play the different characters. A group reading can be very helpful.

I. The Disasters Of Job (Chapters 1-2)
   A. Reasons for troubles
      1. The high purposes of God
      2. The malignant purposes of Satan
   B. The Extent of Job's Troubles Through Satan
      1. The Loss of Job's Property
      2. The Harming of Job's Family
      3. The Turning Away of Job's Friends
II. The Debates of Job and His Friends
                  (Chapter 3:1-42:6)
   A. Job's Cry or Complaint — Ch. 3
   B. Job's Critics — Ch. 4-31
   C. Job's Comforters — Ch. 32-37
   D. Job's Creator — Ch. 38:1-42:6

III. The Deliverance of Job (Chapter 42:1-7)
   A. The Reconciliation
   B. The Restoration

Note: Satan's idea was to test God's child. God was superior and it meant defeat for Satan. So shall it ever be!

It would be good to read the following scriptures with the study of Job: Psalm 37, Psalm 73, Hebrews 12.

AUTHOR

The author is unknown. Authorship is usually attributed to Moses or Solomon. Some scholars think it was Job. Any one of these men would have been knowledgeable about simple and great things, the rich and poor, science, history, and God's creation.

It is written in a poetic style in the original. The first two chapters and the last 10 verses do not use the Jewish poetry.

CHARACTERS

God — The one and only true Lord God Almighty. His abode is in heaven.

Satan — He is a fallen angel. A rebellious one known also as the Devil, who lost his place in heaven. Job 1:7 says he was going about, walking the earth.

Job — Classified as a prophet, he seems to be Hebrew (Jewish) by birth, but Arabian by residence. He lived in the land of Uz (Uts) in Idumea (sometimes called Arabia Petrea).

1. The general opinion is that he is the fifth in descent from Esau. No age is given until after his afflictions. Ch. 42:16, 17

2. Jacob's son, Issachar, had a son named Job. Genesis 46:13

3. In Numbers 26:24 and 1 Chronicles 7:1 he is called Jashub; but no descendants are ever mentioned, making it difficult to trace lineage.

4. In 1 Chronicles 1:35-44 Job is perhaps called Jobab. Depending on language, his name could have been Ayoub.

The Friends of Job

1. **Eliphaz** — came from Tema in Edom, so was called the Temanite. He was a descendant of Esau. Genesis 36:11

2. **Bildad** — The Shuhite, son of Shuah, a descendant of Abraham and Keturah. Genesis 25:2

3. **Zophar** — A Naamathite from the city of Naama in Edom, the south region of Idumea.

4. **Elihu** — A Buzite. Job 32:2. A descendant of Abraham's brother, Nahor. Genesis 22:21. In Jeremiah 25:22 it says Buz was a place in Idumea. The entire region was called Idumea or Arabia Petrea, but since the south district was Edom it made all Job's friends Edomite Arabs. Uz was also located there.

Lamentations talks about Edom or Arabia Petrea. In Jeremiah 49:7 it implies that the Edomites were noted for wisdom and knowledge.

SUBJECT — THE PROBLEM OF PAIN AND SUFFERING

I. The name of Job means 'weeps.' Job 1:1-5. The book begins with a seemingly strange gathering. Compare 1 Kings 22:19-23. About the same as with Micaiah the prophet.

    A. The character of Job established.

        1. Perfect, upright, respected God and avoided evil

        2. Possessions, integrity, importance in the community

II. First encounter or debate between God and Satan (Chapters 1-6)

    A. God allows Satan to exert power (1:12)

        1. To touch Job's property or fortune (1:13-17)

        2. To touch his children (1:18, 19)

    B. Job's faithfulness to God through the first adversity (1:20-22)

III. The second encounter and debate between God and Satan (Chapter 2)

    A. Satan wishes to destroy Job without a cause (v. 1-3)

    B. God replies, "Save his life," but gives Satan permission to afflict. Satan now reveals more of his total pattern for working. He has a totally evil mind. (v. 6)

C. Satan tortures Job's flesh (v. 7)

D. Satan tempts Job's wife (v. 9)

    1. What other areas can he touch then and now?

      a. property-possessions

      b. People-family

      c. Body-flesh

      d. Soul-spirit

E. Job is still faithful to God. He believes that in having for so many years received good from God, he should now also be willing and able to suffer adversities or evil. (v. 10)

F. Three of Job's friends agree together to come and mourn and comfort him. Eliphaz, Bildad and Zophar sat for seven days and seven nights with Job, not speaking, but quietly grieving, mourning and thinking.

IV. Discourses and Debates of Job and His Friends

A. **Job's** cry or complaint (3:2-26)

    1. He rues the day he was born.

    2. He wants to die. He asks, "Why do I have life?"

B. **Eliphaz** replies, begins to remind Job of his good deeds.

    1. He tells of his night visions (4:12-19)

    2. He advises Job that if it were him, he would turn to God (5:8)

    3. He suggests that if Job would repent, his troubles would vanish (5:17-27)

C. **Job** prays to die (6:9); wants sympathy, not reproof (6:14-30); does not understand (7:5), knows he is not wicked, but is covered with worms; the days have no meaning, wants to be alone (7:16)

D. **Bildad** assures Job that God is just. His suffering must be because of much sin. If Job turned to God all will be well (Chapter 8)

E. **Job** replies that God sends punishment on the just and the unjust (9:22); that he is not guilty of evil (10:7); he regrets his birth (10:18-22)

F. **Zophar** tells Job his suffering should be worse because of so much sin (11:5, 6); to put away sin, receive prosperity and happiness again (13-19).

G. **Job** is sarcastic, says he is not inferior to them and wants to speak (12, 13, 14); wicked prosper and righteous suffer (13:13); Questions life after death (14:7-14). If a man dies, will he live again?

H. **Eliphaz** is bitterly sarcastic and angry (15:12).

I. **Job** calls them all miserable comforters (16:2); says he could shake his head, too (16:4); his face is red with weeping and his eyes have rings (16:16); people spit at him and scoff (17:6).

J. **Bildad** tries to frighten Job into repentence (18.)

K. **Job** says that if it is true that he has gone astray, his error remains his concern alone! God's and his! (19:4); He is completely broken, appeals for pity (v. 21); He says emphatically, "I know that my redeemer lives!" His heart yearns to see God (25-27).

> **I know that
> my redeemer lives!
> I will see God!**

L. **Zophar** pictures the fate of the wicked (20;5-29).

M. **Job** agrees, says the wicked are often prosperous, but God is the Almighty (21); "So how can you console me with your nonsense. Nothing is left of your answers but falsehood." (21:34)

N. **Eliphaz** names Job's treatment of the poor as probable cause for his trouble (22).

O. **Job** speaks about his aloneness and bitterness (23, 24); but is confident that when God has tested him he will come forth as gold (v. 10); Is sure he has not disobeyed God's commands (v. 12).

P. **Bildad** very briefly asks how can a man be righteous? He was now done talking! (25)

Q. **Job** is confident, denies sins (26-31); even lists adultery and sun worship, both forbidden. (Compare 31:9-12 with Exodus 20:14, 17 for adultery; 31:26-28 with Deuteronomy 4:19 for idols and sun worship).

Finally all three give up trying to reason with a man trying to justify himself before God. Their intentions may have been good and also redemptive because of their estimation of Job, but they argued on false principles, so their arguments were unconvincing to Job. They really did not know. They had no evidence of Job's wrongdoing.

R. **Elihu** must have heard all the debates, because he was angry with all four men. (23-27) Elihu respected the three men who spoke first, because they were older. He waited until they had finished. By this time he was angry. He thought he had the explanation for all these calamities. He urges Job to humble himself before God, have patience and submit to God's will. He thinks there may be something remedial in Job's sufferings. He rebukes Job (33:12); says God is greater than man (v. 24, 26) and implies correction rather than punishment (37:23 and 33:29, 30)

V. Summary of the Debates

A. Eliphaz suggested Job had sinned and was vain.

B. Bildad inferred and supposed Job to be a sinner and a hypocrite and tries to scare him into repentance.

C. Zophar assumed sin was the direct cause and condemned Job for saying he was innocent. They tried to bring everything to mind that they thought could be the cause. Sin and disobedience of every kind were blamed. Even Job's wife thought all was lost because material wealth was gone. Satan seemed to think Job was serving God for material gain. He struck Job's wealth first! They were all wrong! Only God knew why!

VI. Job's Creator Appears (38:1 — 42:6)

A. God speaks out of a whirlwind and awes Job into silence. He reminds Job of His:

1. Omnipotence — all powerful (42:2)

2. Omniscience — all knowing
3. Omnipresence — present everywhere
    a. Job says he is unworthy
    b. If Job could not understand God's rulings or workings in the natural realm, how much less could he understand the moral and spiritual?
B. Job's Deliverance (42:1-17)
    1. Reconciliation (1-5). Job was now in a situation where he wanted to be many times previous to this during his uncommon sufferings. (10:2, 13:3, 18:23, 19:7, 23:3-10, 31:35-37) He wanted to ask God "Why this? Why me? Why so much?" But when God spoke, Job saw himself more clearly. He saw his own smallness and God's greatness. He saw enough, heard enough and cared enough to submit to God totally and with victory.
    2. Repentance (v. 6). Job repents, "I despise myself and repent in dust and ashes." So overwhelmed with love and respect and sorrow, he forgot to ask WHY?
    3. Job's Restoration (42:7-17)
        a. Job's three friends were rebuked for speaking wrongly about God. They were commanded to sacrifice. Elihu was not included. (v. 7)
        b. Job acts as intercessor for them and his prayer is accepted (v. 9)
        c. Job's patience was rewarded by a blessing (v. 10-17)
            (1) He received double of all possessions he was forced to lose.
            (2) A new family, along with former relatives and friends, came to associate with him.
            (3) Job was accepted and blessed so that his "latter days were better than his first days."
VII. A reference to Patience
A. In James 5:10, 11 is direct reference to Job's patience. "Brothers, as an example of patience in the face of suffering, take the prophets who spoke in the name of the Lord. As you know, we consider blessed those

who have persevered. You have heard of Job's perseverance and have seen what the Lord finally brought about.
The Lord is full of compassion and mercy."

VIII. Thoughts on Job's suffering and Patience. Job was a
righteous man who served God. God knew he could be trust-
ed and faithful. He would have allowed none other to be chosen
for such unusual suffering. He does not allow a faithful child
with a heart that is righteous to be lost to Satan — tried
perhaps, but not lost. If anyone is lost it is of his own choosing. Even though Job was "perfect" he found himself to be
loathsome in God's sight. He was never given a reason for his
suffering. But he did know that to trust God in all areas of
life is most necessary.

We have a sovereign God. A wise God. His wisdom is above
and beyond our human mind to understand. Romans 11:33
says, "Oh, the depth of the riches of the wisdom and
knowledge of God. How unsearchable are His judgments and
His ways past finding out."

The patience of Job is a big help as an example in dealing
with suffering. It serves to answer questions for individuals
and the church.

Sometimes it is necessary to ask "Why?"

But more important is to ask — "What does God want
to say to me?" Or, "I am at this point in life now. Where
do I go from here?"

If we dwell too much on the whys, it could be mind shat-
tering, because, like Job, we may not ever know why. Perhaps
there are cases where there is direct evidence of sin in a life,
causing sickness and suffering.

As believers we need to trust God's judgment, exercise faith,
be submissive and victorious. We must "rejoice with those that
do rejoice and weep with those that weep."

But we cannot afford to suppose or speculate about another
person's guilt or innocence when we do not know the heart.

Concerning questions about which the Bible is silent — like
why God allows Satan to do evil, or where a passage may not
be clear, or we have no insight about it — then we must be

silent and not suppose, imagine or speculate. We may sin by doing so or cause someone else to sin.

One thing is very clear throughout the Bible. God is the Creator of all things. He is in control of all things and He knows the hearts of men.

In Isaiah 45:5, 6, 7, God says to Cyrus that He, God, is the Sovereign Lord, and that Cyrus should trust his judgment. "I am the Lord and there is no other; apart from me there is no God. I will strengthen you, though you have not acknowledged me. So that from the rising of the sun to the place of its setting men may know there is none beside me. I am the Lord and there is no other. I form the light and create darkness. I bring prosperity and create disaster (evil, KJV). I the Lord do all these things."

In Amos 3:1-6 comparisons are made to remind people that God is in control — but there is punishment for sin. "Shall a trumpet be blown in the city and the people be not afraid? Shall there be evil in the city and the Lord hath not done it?" Verse 6.

God is in control over everything. How comforting and awesome!

Satan could not have worked his evil on Job without the expressed permission of God. Satan still can go no further than God allows.

So if sickness, pain, suffering and adversities of all kinds come upon us because of original sin being passed to the human race through Adam and Eve, then we can surely know God allows it. Satan's influence was used in the temptation and fall of Adam and Eve. Eve chose to disobey first and then Adam also chose to sin.

IX. Historical notes

A. No date can be given as to the exact time when Job lived. But because of the way Job observed the burnt offerings, it seems he lived after the law was given on Mount Sinai to Moses and the children of Israel. Job knew the law. He offered the offering prescribed for sins committed through ignorance. He said, "If my children have committed sins."

B. For specific other references about offerings and the law, see:

Leviticus 4:1-35, 5:15-19

Numbers 24-29

Job 1:5 — Job sanctified his children and offered burnt offerings daily.

Leviticus 9:7 and 22 — It was meant to be observed.

Exodus 29:38-42

Numbers 28:3, 6, 10, 15, 24, 31

Ezra 3:5 — Ezra kept it after the captivity.

Nehemiah 10:33 — Nehemiah offered burnt offerings daily.

C. Historians say that with the final destruction of Jerusalem in 70 A.D., the Edomites disappeared from history just as Obadiah, the prophet, predicted in vs. 10, 16, 18. In vs. 17, 19, 21, he says Judah would prevail. This prophecy was fulfilled.

X. Other scriptures that refer to Job

A. Ezekiel 14:14-20 — Job is first mentioned by the prophet who considers Job's standing equal to that of Noah and Daniel.

B. Proverbs 3:11 — Despise not the chastening.

C. Hebrews 12:5 — Despise not the chastening.

D. Job 5:17 — Despise not the chastening.

E. Romans 2:11 — Discusses respect of persons. Compare with Job 34:18, 19 in regard for rich and poor.

F. 1 Timothy 6:7 — brought nothing into the world. Compare with Job 1:21. "Naked came I . . ."

G. James 5:11 refers to the patience of Job.

XI. Summary

A. God is a sovereign Lord.

B. He is the Creator and Ruler over all His creation.

C. The faithful righteous believers are never forgotten by God — even though they are or may be suffering and oppressed. They can have victory over adversaries by having faith that what God promises to do, He is able to do. This brings peace within.

D. The disobedient, the unbeliever, and the wicked may be prosperous or suffer. They may seem to rule and influence their world things for a time, but they can never have peace or be victorious at the end.

E. Neither the faithful nor the disobedient will be ultimately punished or rewarded here on this earth.

1. Those who follow after worldly things, the things Satan uses to deceive people, will have eternal damnation and rejection. Nothing to do, no place to go, nothing to see and hear but eternal misery of the worst kind. Job only had a hint of it.

2. But those who trust Him with their lives will have eternal joy and peace. The believer's suffering here is only temporary. Then rejoicing. When Jesus was on the cross, He suffered physically, mentally and spiritually: physically by dying slowly, mentally by the trauma of waiting and the shame, spiritually by taking our sins and knowing God had forsaken Him. He and we can become one in suffering.

"If we suffer with Him we shall reign with Him." This entails many and varied sufferings for Christ's sake. The whole Book of Job is a lesson on patient endurance in suffering. In the end we will be rewarded by seeing God.

In
the
beginning
was
the Word
and the Word was
with God, and the
Word was God.

Chapter IV
Healing In The New Testament

In the New Testament many healings are recorded.

Physical and spiritual healings were performed by Jesus and the apostles. Demoniacs and people with varying sicknesses were healed. Dead persons were raised to life.

Jesus did his healing works in a period of about three years. This was also a preparation period for the apostles He had called to help Him. He gave them instruction in teaching the truth so that when he would leave them for the cross they could continue the message of redemption for all people.

They were given power and authority to take over when Jesus was crucified and died. When He rose from the dead He claimed victory over death. When He ascended to heaven He kept His word. After He was glorified, Jesus received the Spirit to send to the believers living in a sick earthly world.

For their ministry the apostles were granted (KJV) signs and wonders or they were enabled (NIV) to do signs and wonders. Acts 14:3. It was not natural for the apostles to do these miracles on their own. They were given this power to: 1) Confirm the Word, 2) Work by the power of the Spirit of God. Romans 15:19, and 3) For a demonstration of the Spirit and power of God. 1 Corinthians 2:4.

Hebrews 2:1-4 says, "This salvation was first announced by the Lord, was confirmed to us by those who heard him. God also testified to it by signs and wonders and various miracles, and gifts of the Holy Spirit distributed according to His will."

Let us review the sickness and suffering in the New Testament and see what method was used for healing or cleansing and why the contact.

1. Matthew 8:1-4. Jesus cleansed a leper. In speaking about leprosy, the scriptures used the term cleansed, a washing process.

Just as a sinner needs a spiritual cleansing by God, the lepers were thought to need a double cleansing by God.

This particular leper said to Jesus, "If you will, you can make me clean."

Jesus said with authority, "I will." In an unusual gesture, he touched the leper and said, "For giving a testimony to the priests."

He kept the law by doing this. The cured man was not to tell it to everyone because people were looking for an earthly king and Jesus did not want to be involved in such a movement.

2. Matthew 8:5-13. A centurion's servant was healed. It was not the faith of the sick servant, but the centurion's faith that was great. God's mercy was equal to and superior to this faith. Jesus only needed to speak and the servant was healed.

3. Matthew 8:14-17. Peter's mother-in-law was sick with a fever. She was healed when Jesus touched her. She thought clearly and was willing to serve immediately.

4. Matthew 9:2-8. A paralytic (palsied) man was healed. Pardon took place before health here, as it says in Psalm 103:3, "Who forgives all your iniquities, who heals all your diseases."

The unbelieving scribes thought Jesus was blaspheming — attributing to Himself the things only God could do. They thought His power was from Satan.

We need to notice three proofs of His Deity here.

a. Jesus knew their thoughts.

b. He forgave sins.

c. He restored health.

It was equally easy for Jesus to speak any of the three words 'forgive,' 'be healed' or 'arise, go.' As the Son of God he had this unlimited power from God. Only God can forgive sin.

As the man obeyed, the people looking on glorified God. Jesus said, "It was done so they would know that the Son of Man has power to forgive sins."

5. Matthew 9:20-22. A woman with an issue of blood was healed because of her faith. In the Mark 5 account of the healing, it says she spent all her money on doctors, but continued to get worse before she came to Jesus.

6. Matthew 9:27-31. Two blind men came to Jesus for mercy. Jesus asked them, "Do you believe I am able?" They replied, "Yes, Lord," and expressed faith. Jesus touched and healed them.

7. Matthew 12:9-13. A man with a withered hand was in the synagogue on the Sabbath Day. The man stretched out his hand by the command of Jesus and was healed. This was belief only. Jesus knew the thoughts of the critics about doing good on the Sabbath. The law said no, but grace said yes.

8. Mark 7:31-37. A deaf and dumb man was brought to Jesus for healing. Jesus took him aside, spit, touched, prayed and healed him. He charged the people to keep quiet about it, but they disobeyed. To them He was only a healer, and not particularly the Son of God.

9. Mark 8:22-26. Jesus led a blind man at Bethsaida outside the city. Jesus touched the man's eyes with spittle. He asked if he could see, then touched the man the second time. He charged the man not to go to the city, but to go home healed.

10. Luke 13:10-17. A woman had an infirmity for 18 years. Jesus said Satan had her bound for 18 years. A slave to Satan, she was an unbeliever. Jesus healed her on the Sabbath in the synagogue. There was no faith on her part, only the compassion of Jesus, His touch and His words.

11. Luke 14:1-6. A man with dropsy was healed on the Sabbath in a Pharisee's house. Jesus touched him and sent him away.

12. Luke 17:11-19. Ten lepers on the way to Jerusalem were healed. Only one returned to say thanks.

Giving thanks is very important and commanded in all situations.

Jesus told the one leper, "Your faith has made you well. Go, show yourselves to the priests." This would have been for proper wholeness. Jesus kept the law here, for when a diseased leper was forced out of society only the priest could pronounce him clean or healed.

Leprosy, being emblematic of sin, was only made whole by God. Jesus was here sending a message to the priests through this leper. He was expressing His Deity.

13. Mark 10:46-52 and Luke 18:35-43. Blind Bartimaeus asked mercy and sight of Jesus. Jesus spoke the word; Bartimaeus had faith and received his sight.

14. Luke 22:50-51. Malchus' ear was cut off. Jesus touched and healed it. Whether the ear was put back on or whether the wound only was healed, or whether he formed a new ear, we are not told. The point is, Jesus healed the enemy and rebuked the objecting disciples. John 18:10.

15. John 4:43-54. A nobleman's son at Capernaum was healed. Jesus said, "Your son will live." Jesus was sad because people wanted signs and wonders. Later the nobleman believed what Jesus said.

16. John 5:1-16. An impotent (invalid in some way) man in Jerusalem was infirm for 38 years. He had no faith of himself. Jesus healed him on the Sabbath. Notice the following points:

    a. Jesus knew the man inside out.

    b. In verse 14 Jesus told the man to stop sinning lest a worse thing would come upon him; stop rejecting Christ and believe on Him. In verse 19 Jesus confirms His Father.

    c. Verse 28, 29 says those who reject Christ keep on sinning and will be condemned. This is the whole picture.

    d. The healed man told the Jews that it was Jesus who did this for him. He had not admitted nor known this before.

    e. It does not say the multitude of other impotent people were healed.

17. John 9:1-7. A man was born blind at Jerusalem. This was a congenital blindness, not mentally or emotionally produced. Jesus used spittle, made a mud plaster and put it on the man's eyes, then told him to wash in the pool of Siloam. The man knew his way to the pool without his sight and obeyed. He came back seeing.

This was again on the Sabbath. The man expressed no faith in the Son of God at the first meeting. The disciples asked, "Who sinned? This man or his parents, that he was born blind?" Jesus said, "Neither this man nor his parents, but this happened so that the work of God might be displayed in his life." This is a very plain statement of purpose.

When the Pharisees started to bring charges to prove who this man was declaring or talking about, he answered, "One thing I know, I was blind, but now I see." He did not know who Jesus really was. The man was thrown out of the synagogue.

Later, when Jesus revealed Himself to the man, he said, "Lord, I believe." And he worshipped Jesus. He really had testified of the One who saved him and saves us as well, and heals us continually.

There were many other needy people in Jerusalem, Galilee, Syria, Genesaret and Judea; there were great multitudes and all manner of diseases. There were times, though, when Jesus went away from crowds of people or even sent them away from Him.

1. Matthew 14:23. Jesus dismissed the people so He could be alone.

2. Matthew 26:36-39. Jesus was at Gethsemane before His crucifixion. He prayed there alone.

3. Mark 1:38. He arose early in the morning and went to a solitary place to pray.

4. Mark 6:31-32. Jesus went to a quiet place to rest; there were too many people and He had no chance to eat.

5. Luke 8:23. He was asleep in a boat when a storm arose.

6. Luke 6:12. He prayed all night alone before choosing the apostles.

Usually there seemed to be an endless stream of sick and sinful people for Him to meet. Jesus was the Son of God, but also the Son of man and had needs that you and I have.

Great and
marvelous are
your deeds,
Lord God Almighty.
Just and true are
your ways,
King of the Ages.

Chapter V
Healing Of Sorrow For Death

Sometimes we forget that sorrow and grief after a death are included in a healing wholeness plan. A brief review tells us Jesus thought it was important to help heal broken hearts. He demonstrated this visibly in three specific examples given in the Bible. This was a special healing for a suffering sorrow after a death. It was also to show the glory of God through the action.

1. Matthew 9:18-26 Jairus' daughter died and was raised to life. Jairus had faith. Jesus touched her and spoke to her. Only God's power can raise to life.

2. Luke 7:11-15 A widow's son at Nain was raised to life. With compassion Jesus touched and spoke to the widow's son who was being carried out on a bier or coffin. He said to the widow, "Don't cry." To the son He said, "Young man, get up." No person had asked for help or restoration. Jesus is full of compassion and mercy.

3. John 11:1-46 Lazarus was dead and already entombed at Bethany. Jesus prayed and called, "Come forth." This was a sickness Lazarus had "not unto death," but that the glory of God would be demonstrated.

Matthew 27:50-54 cites a very powerful display of God's care for His faithful people. When Jesus died graves were opened and many Holy people were raised to life.

We also have the example of the glorious resurrection of Jesus after His own death. Matthew 28, Mark 16, Luke 24 and John 20 tell us about the resurrection of Jesus.

What a victory!

The need for healing during a grieving period after a death touches everyone at some particular time.

There should be no bitterness or resentment in a time of sorrow for a committed child of God. If bitter and resentful traits are active, it is very unhealthy.

88

In sorrow and distress we sometimes may think and do as it says in Lamentations 1:12. "Is it nothing to you who pass by? Look around and see. Is any suffering like my suffering that was inflicted on me? . . ."

We allow self pity to overcome us. We may recognize God's hand in the situation but we strike back. We allow the sorrow to overcome us. 2 Corinthians 2:7 says, ". . . overwhelmed by excessive sorrow."

Then it becomes a real challenge for a Christian believer to help that person and affirm them in love. I Thessalonians 4:13 tells us not to grieve as those "who have no hope." We grieve as those who have hope.

It is true that each person's sorrow varies because of personality differences, emotional shock, and spiritual health.

The remedy may be what Jesus told His disciples in the Garden of Gethsemane. Jesus had been in prayer suffering alone. He had told the disciples to wait for Him. The disciples were ". . . exhausted from sorrow." Luke 22:45. Jesus told them, "Get up and pray so that you will not fall into temptation."

Matthew 11:28 says, "Come to me, all you who are weary and burdened and I will give you rest."

Psalm 147:3 says, "The Lord heals the broken hearted and binds up their wounds."

Matthew 5:4 says, "Blessed are they that mourn: for they shall be comforted."

Ecclesiastes 7:3 says, "Sorrow is better than laughter, because a sad face is good for the heart."

An untitled and anonymous poem also speaks about sorrow:

> I walked a mile with Pleasure,
>   She chatted with me all the way,
> But I was none the wiser
>   For what she had to say.
> I walked a mile with Sorrow,
>   And ne'er a word said she,
> But O, the things I learned from her
>   When Sorrow walked with me.

Sorrow and grief affect people differently, but it definitely takes a healing process to again restore them.

If they have allowed themselves to become physically sick, that, too, needs to be dealt with.

Healing is available for all sorrows if we make the conditions right for receiving it.

Blessed be the name of our Lord Jesus Christ.

The Lord
is full of
Compassion and
mercy.

Chapter VI
Demonics Healed

When we speak of healing we tend to think mostly of the physically sick, organically or functionally sick people.

We must also remember the mentally and emotionally sick and those who have evil spirits, because this affects the whole body. No medicine can cure demon possession. God can. Mental or emotional illness is often caused by fear. Fear of fear, fear of self, or fear of the unknown. Sometimes it may begin with a physical problem. Let us look at some examples.

The Bible says in Matthew 8:28-34 that the Gadarene demoniacs lived in tombs. They knew Jesus to be the Son of God. When Jesus was going to heal the man whose body had been invaded by demons, the demons begged Jesus to allow them to go into a herd of swine nearby. The demons wanted to enter the swine because there would have been no resistance. A person would have wanted to resist.

The demons did not want to go to their final awful place. They could not leave by themselves. God permitted this unusual request and the demons and swine rushed over a cliff into the sea. It was really an unnatural happening as these were probably Jews and should not have had swine. It is a story of mercy and justice. The rage of evil is shown and of what little value is material gain in the wrong hands.

Matthew 9:32-35 speaks about a dumb person who was also demon possessed. The demon was cast out by the power of God. It was unusual and the people said, ''It was never so seen in Israel.'' The word spread. This would have been proof and fulfillment of the prophecy in Isaiah 35:5, 6 that the Messiah had come in the flesh.

In Matthew 12:22-34 a blind, dumb and demonic man was healed by Jesus when there was belief in a man only. The Pharisees questioned if it could be Jesus who healed him. Jesus knew their thoughts and said to them, "Can Satan cast out Satan? Can he be divided against himself?"

Think on this and reread the whole story. Just as Satan cannot drive out Satan, neither can "self" cast out "self." There can be no deliverance for a sinner apart from Jesus Christ. We cannot be safe in our own strength.

In Matthew 15:21-28 the Syro-Phoenician's daughter was healed through the faith of the mother.

Matthew 17:14-21 gives the account of the healing of an epileptic, lunatic boy. Jesus rebuked the demon when the disciples could not. This was a special healing — by prayer and fasting only. The disciples were rebuked for unbelief.

In Mark 1:34 Jesus healed many sick and demon possessed. He would not let the demons tell who He was.

Demons always know who Jesus is. Jesus knew it was not yet His Father's appointed time for Him to be crucified. There were too many political controversies about Him setting up an earthly kingdom of which He wanted no part. He was interested in a spiritual kingdom. He wanted to establish heart relationships before He was crucified.

Mark 1:23-26 says that in the synagogue at Capernaum there was a man with an evil spirit. The demon knew who Jesus was, but Jesus told him, "Be quiet and come out of him." The evil spirit shrieked as he left the body of the man.

News of Jesus spread as a result of this. It was a demonstration of Jesus' power over evil and His compassion for a man who did not ask for help. Even today some may be healed who do not ask. Jesus came "to destroy the works of the devil." 1 John 3:8. He does this by His almighty goodness and justice. He also came to save people from their sins and deliver them from the results of sin.

Josephus, a Jewish historian, wrote, "There was not a nation under heaven more wicked than Judea in Christ's time. They were addicted to magic and invited evil spirits to be familiar with them."

How utterly depraved and sick! Steeped in sin! Could this be why Jesus chose these particular healing signs and wonders?

Was it to demonstrate His power and clarify His identity? What is the world doing today, and do we as believers give consent?

The fact of sin is not determined by our environment. There is sin. But where and how we live will simply determine the way in which we will sin.

One of the greatest indications of human sin and depravity is ignorance and indifference toward the love of God. Ignorance because persons have not heard of His love or do not care, and indifference because of willfulness.

Could some of us who live more sheltered lives not know about the violence and crime that causes unrest of the soul in so many people? Could we be caught in the judgment because we have become inactive or passive and turned our eyes and ears away from these events? Are we doing anything to change these situations? Lord have mercy on us!

We have a declining national morality, an educational battleground, a menace of AIDS, a fatal disease called pornography, a holocaust of abortions, a plague of promiscuity, homosexuality. Entertainment screams sex, lewdness and violence. Are we consenting to evil? Woe! Woe! Woe!

But God is love and can heal these evils if we ask.

The organization of Satan and evil spirits is another topic — the total invasion of a personality and its effects. We will only look at a few ideas to point out that only God's power can heal a demonic person.

C. S. Lewis wrote in the preface to *The Screwtape Letters*, "There are two equal and opposite errors into which our race can fall about devils:

"One is to disbelieve in their existence.

"One is to believe and feel an excessive and unhealthy interest in them."

Because of the mystery involved concerning the unknown, we have a tendency to speculate. We can become confused and lose the right way. Evil is not a fantasy. It is real. When we are in unfavorable situations or have become lax in our spiritual lives, Satan will try to strike. We must use extreme caution and keep our minds and hearts healthy toward Jesus Christ.

We cannot close our minds to the fact of sin. There is sin! There is distress and evil all around us that can contribute to making an unhealthy heart and mind. What we should do is open the mind to receive what is wholesome and fills us full. A healthy mind must exercise some control and even censor its intake. Otherwise it would become diseased and our thoughts not balanced. It could retain nothing of value.

To illustrate, we should open our minds for the same reason we open our mouths to eat something worth swallowing and make it a part of ourselves. Our minds are fragile and yet very lively and elastic to instruction and feeding. What do we ingest and digest?

The late V. Raymond Edman of Wheaton College said, "There are many who know the Saviour as their own but are un-instructed in the Word of God so as to be strangers to the reality of spiritual warfare. Such know the gospel to save from sin but not the authority of the name of the Lord Jesus Christ against Satan and his hosts.

There are many Christians born again of the Spirit of God, who are unfamiliar with spiritual realities either good or evil . . . . The Spirit is not a living dynamic personality to them, nor are demonic personalities a reality because such believers lack discernment of things spiritual."

There are many, though, who are acquainted with the indwelling presence of the Holy Spirit, who know God as Father and the Son as a redeemer. They know what spiritual warfare is and are constantly better preparing themselves for God's service in testifying for Christ against the works of Satan.

"Demonic activity is not uniform the world over nor in historical experience." V. Raymond Edman.

We sometimes smile at horoscopes or at fortune tellers, mediums and other similar individuals, not realizing what all is involved. Many of us have really not been in a position to see the devastating effects of their actions in a presonal way or we would not smile about materialism, occultism, black magic, white magic, magical and criminal hypnosis, readers, palmistry, astrology, horoscopes and all kinds of spiritist phenomena, seances, Ouija boards, and many phenomena that are works that Satan uses in his deceitfulness. They all seem to be an attempt to rule the mind through extrasensory means. We even need to be careful of new games on the market, how we use them or allow our children to use them.

The children of Israel were surrounded by these influences, having recently come from the Egypt described in the Old Testament. The Lord gave instructions against involvement in these in:

Leviticus 20:6 and 27.

Deuteronomy 18:10-12

1 Chronicles 10:13

Jeremiah 29:8, 9

We have an example in Acts 16:16-18 when Paul is confronted by the fortune telling slave girl. In Revelation 21:8 the Word says, "All these shall be in the lake that burns with fire and brimstone." There are so many works of power and intrigue so closely linked to demon possession that it is important not to touch or dabble with them. We of ourselves cannot sometimes distinguish between them. Only with God's help is it possible. God help us in this evil world!

The people who have had experiences in this terrible trouble know the despair of a ravaged, demon possessed person. They have had contact with the powers of darkness and know the joy and transformation of God's delivering power. We must believe Jesus and the experiences related by others in delivering from evil a miserable body bound by Satan. We need to heed the advice of Ephesians 6:10-18, to "put on the full armor of God so that you can take your full stand against the devil's schemes" and be strong in faith in Christ.

It would be wise if we do not go after the sensational healings or healers. They sometimes get closely linked to demonic works. Satan has been known to effect some healing on a person in some cases, but always some worse affliction comes upon the person.

An example from a case file recounted in *Between Christ and Satan* by Kurt Koch, that in Germany a woman needed to have her leg amputated. She wanted to save her leg, so she visited a magic charmer without a doctor's knowledge. This charmer told her she would have to believe in him if she wanted to be healed. He held a magic charm and repeated the Lord's prayer three times. The woman's pain vanished and her leg was saved. The doctors were puzzled. Later, however, the woman began to suffer from various psychic disturbances and her family became accident prone. Satanic oppression often causes suffering.

We need to steer clear of anything which does not follow scriptural teaching. Satan always intends evil, but God intends good. What God says is the truth. We need to search the Word of God. So many learning surprises await us as we read and study His Word and understand it more clearly. We never go wrong with the word of God. He gave us a reliable book to read.

Satan does not have one book as such, although a follower of his published what he calls a Satanic Bible. What a chilling thought! Many Biblical mockeries, distorted and confusing thoughts are written under Satan's influence. They are disguised as angels of light, to deceive, entice and persuade a person to act and speak under the name of religion when they really are not religious. Satan is interested in the seduction of believers, and holding onto the unbeliever.

We need to exercise daily our love, compassion, reason, and keen discernment. Exercise faith in God and trust His judgments, use wisdom, use the council of Christians. We dare not dwell on the cults or strange and different gatherings, but we surely must be aware of them. They are dangerously near and very subtle.

We want to be prepared with God's armor, the Word of God, at all times. When once we give ourselves over to Satan, he can make us do anything he wants. God gives us a choice. The farther away we get from the image of God, the more and more we grow like Satan and are unaware of it.

It takes a special gift of discernment and healing to cast out an evil spirit. Jesus always cast out demons by command.

Not everyone is qualified and gifted to work in this area. Not everyone is qualified to work in the area of mental or emotional sickness, or occultism. Without the power of God resting on us for this work, we are helpless. It is of utmost importance to keep our minds stayed on Christ, our lives full of the Spirit of God, leaving no room for evil.

I pray that we will always stay within God's loving care so that we do not get into a situation where evil can creep in and develop to overpower us and hold us until we become damned for eternity. God save us from such an awful destiny!

But thanks be to God. He gives us the victory through our Lord Jesus Christ, when we are sick or well. We can live daily with encouragement and hope in Jesus Christ our Lord.

Chapter VII

Charts:
Parallel Accounts Of Healings

Healings By Jesus

	Matthew	Mark	Luke	John
A leper	8:1-4	1:40-45	5:12-16	
Centurian's servant	8:5-13		7:1-10	
Peter's mother-in-law	8:14-17	1:29-31	4:38-39	
A paralytic	9:2-8	2:1-12	5:17-26	
Woman with issue of blood	9:20-22	5:25-34	8:43-48	
Two blind men	9'27-31			
Nobleman's son at Capernaum				4:43-54
Impotent man for 38 years at Jerusalem				5:1-16
Deaf and dumb man		7:31-37		
Blind man at Bethsaida		8:22-26		
One born blind at Jerusalem				9:1-7
Woman 18 yr. infirmity			13:10-17	
Man with dropsy			14:1-6	
Ten lepers			17:11-19	
Lazarus the beggar			16:19-31	
Blind Bartimaeus	20:29-34	10:46-52	18:35-43	
Malchus' ear	26:51	14:47	22:50-51	18:10
Many in Jerusalem	8:16	1:32	4:30	2:23
Galilee — Syria — all manner	4:23-24		6:17-19	
Various towns	9:35	3:7-12	13:32	
Genesaret	14:34-36	6:53-56		
Borders of Judea	19:1-2		7:21-22	
Great Multitudes	15:30-31			
Withered hand	12:9-13	3:1-6	6:6-11	
Lazarus				11:1-17
Many others				21:25

Demoniacs Healed By Jesus

	Matthew	Mark	Luke	John	Acts
Many healed with a word	8:16-17		4:40, 41		
Gadarenes and swine	8:28-34	5:1-20	8:26-39		
Blind, dumb and demoniac	12:22-34	3:11	11:14-16		
Dumb, unclean	9:32-34				
Syro-Phoenician's daughter	15:21-28	7:24-30			
Epileptic or lunatic boy	17:14-21	9:14-29	9:39-43		
Many devils		1:32-34			
Others				21:25	
At Capernaum in the synagogue		1:23-26	4:33-36		

Raising From The Dead

	Matthew	Mark	Luke	John	Acts
Jairus' daughter	9:18-26	5:22-43	8:41-56		
Widow's son at Nain			7:11-15		
Lazarus at Bethany				11:1-46	

Healings By The Apostles

	Matthew	Mark	Luke	John
Peter and the cripple at the temple				3:1-16
Peter's shadow at Jerusalem				5:12-16
Paul's conversion — blindness				9:1-19
Aeneas, paralytic				9:32-35
Dorcas raised from dead				9:36-43

Healings By The Apostles

	Matthew	Mark	Luke	John
Impotent man's feet				14:1-10
Slave girl				
fortune teller				16:16
Seven sons of Sceva				19:13-20

	Matthew	Mark	Luke	John	Acts
Special miracles					19:11-12
Eutychus					20:7-12
Publius and Paul					28:1-10
Timothy	1 Tim. 5:23 1 Tim. 5:7-10				

Paul's sufferings and the Apostles beginning in Acts Admonition of James to the Church — James 1-5

Chapter VIII
The "Acts" Of The Apostles

To help us understand healing, it is important to look at the list of the "Acts" of the Apostles when the church began.

Acts 3:1-16 — Peter and John and the cripple are at the temple. The cripple had no faith, but Peter touched him and spoke to him. He exercised faith and compassion. The man was healed.

Acts 5:12-16 — Peter and the apostles healed all in the area.

Acts 6:8 — Stephen did signs and wonders.

Acts 8:5-13 — Philip spoke and performed healings. Even a sorcerer became a believer. "Faith cometh by hearing, and hearing by the word of God."

Acts 9:1-19 — Saul was struck with blindness for several days. Saul will be discussed in more detail later. Saul is later called Paul (Acts 13:9).

Acts 9:32-35 — Aeneas, a paralytic, was bedfast for eights years, but was healed through Peter's faith in God. He said, "Jesus Christ heals you." He gave testimony correctly, taking no glory to himself.

Acts 9:36-43 — Dorcas, a disciple, was raised alive from the dead. Peter prayed, spoke, and touched her. Many believed in Christ because of this miracle.

Acts 13:11 — Paul used God's power and struck Elymas, the sorcerer, with blindness.

Acts 14:1-10 — An impotent man, crippled in his feet since birth, heard preaching and believed. Peter understood the man's faith and by command from Peter, Jesus healed him.

Acts 16:16-18 — A slave girl fortune teller pestered Paul and his friends many days by following them and yelling after them. Paul did not cast out the evil spirit immediately, but it grieved him and he finally cast it out.

Acts 19:11-12 — God did extraordinary healing by using handkerchiefs and aprons blessed by Paul.

Acts 19:13-25 — Seven sons of Sceva were overcome by an evil spirit while practicing an exorcism falsely. A frightening experience! The evil spirits prompted the man in whom they lived to overcome and fight them. The seven sons were wounded and fled the house. Because of this, people confessed their sins, believed God, and sorcerers quit their business. The word of God spread greatly and He was magnified.

Acts 20:7-12 — Eutychus went to sleep and fell out of a third story window and died. Paul restored him.

Acts 28:1-6 — A viper fastened itself to Paul's hand. Paul was kept by God's power, for the viper did Paul no harm.

Acts 28:1-10 — Publius' faither-in-law was sick and Paul prayed for him and touched him to bring about healing. Many others were healed because of this.

2 Corinthians 11 and 12 discusses Paul's many sufferings as a man of God, his "thorn" in the flesh. He says in 12:2-5, "I know a man in Christ who fourteen years ago was caught up to the third heaven. Whether it was in the body or out of the body I do not know — God knows. And I know that this man — whether in the body or apart from the body I do not know, but God knows — was caught up to Paradise. He heard inexpressible things, things that man is not permitted to tell. I will boast about a man like that, but I will not boast about myself, except about my weakness." But he refrained so no one would think more highly of him than they ought. He said, "To keep me from becoming conceited because of these surpassingly great revelations, there was given me a thorn in my flesh, a messenger of Satan to torment me."

Paul's "thorn" has been the subject of much discussion with various points of view.

Some publicly acclaimed healers in today's world insist that Paul's thorn was not a physical thing. They claim this because Paul was not relieved even after praying about it. They suggest his thorn was false teachers. This would have been Satan's work. Matthew 13:19 says, "When someone hears the

Word and doesn't understand, then Satan comes and takes away what was sown in the hearts.'' Let us think about this. Paul had been carrying this thorn for fourteen years, but had been converted and preaching before that time. There were opposing forces at work from the beginning of his ministry. There were word stoppers and false teachers, so it could not have been outside influences.

Paul says in Romans 8:35-39, "Who shall separate us from the love of Christ. Shall tribulation or distress or persecution or famine, or nakedness, or peril, or sword? As it is written, for Thy sake we are killed all day long; we are accounted as sheep for the slaughter. No in all these things we are more than conquerors through Him that loved us. For I am persuaded that neither death, not life, nor angels, nor principalities, nor powers, nor things present, nor things to come, nor height, nor depth nor any other creature shall be able to separate us from the love of God.''

Many people tried to separate Paul from the love of God. Today there are also many influences that could separate a Christian from the love of Christ, but we need not let that happen. We can choose to be a follower of Him just as Paul chose to follow Him.

Paul wrote in Galatians 4:13-15, "As you know, it was because of an illness that I first preached the the gospel to you. Even though my illness was a trial to you, you did not treat me with contempt or scorn. Instead, you welcomed me as if I were Christ Jesus himself. (KJV v. 14, "And my temptation which was in my flesh you despised not, nor rejected; but received me as an angel of God, even as Christ Jesus.") What has happened to your joy? I can testify that, if you could have done so, you would have torn out your eyes and given them to me.''

In Galatians 6:11 Paul says about his writing, "See what large letters I use as I write to you with my own hand.'' It implies here that by using large letters he was able to do his own writing. He often had to dictate to a helper. This says Paul did have an infirmity and it cannot be denied.

Why eyes? Why not eyes? Either way, this thorn was given to Paul personally, for a particular purpose. "To keep me from becoming conceited because of these surpassingly great revelations, there was given me a thorn in my flesh, a messenger of Satan, to torment me. Three times I pleaded with the Lord to take it away from me. But He said to me, My grace is sufficient for you, for my power is made perfect in weakness. Therefore I will boast all the more gladly about my weaknesses, so that Christ's power may rest on me."

This says it could not have been spiritual weaknesses, mental or emotional, so it would have had to be physical, in the flesh, not sin nor sinfulness.

God wills for us sufficient strength to carry out His plan. He gives power according to need. He can use every person in proportion as they allow His spirit to work in their lives, and how well it will reflect His image. Paul knew that to be strong in the Lord was the most important thing. He was not healed in this particular physical area.

In Acts 9 when Paul was still called Saul and, as an unbeliever was zealously persecuting Christians, God struck him with blindness. He stayed blind for three days. The Lord was able to restore Saul's sight with just a word, but He did not. He chose the ministry of a believer to manifest His presence. In verses 15 and 16 the Lord told Ananias, "Go, this man is my chosen instrument to carry my name before the Gentiles and their kings and before the people of Israel. I will show him how much he must suffer for my name."

God sent Ananias to lay hands on Paul to receive sight and to be filled with the Holy Spirit. Paul arose, was baptized, ended his fast and spent several days with the disciples. Then at once he began preaching that Jesus was the Son of God and had brought salvation. He was now regenerate.

Read Galatians, chapter 1. Verse 15 says God had set Paul apart from birth and called him by His grace to reveal Jesus to the Gentile nations. Paul was now in a frame of mind where God could use him best: humble, submissive and still zealous.

Through all the many contacts and sufferings of every kind — shipwrecks, stripes, infirmities, imprisonments, oppositions — God's grace was sufficient to keep Paul faithful and victorious. Paul did not become bitter nor blame God unjustly for not healing him, even though he prayed three times to have the "thorn" removed. He accepted God's decision in this matter and continued in his work, being obedient to death. It would be right for him to pray many times about his preaching and for his helpers, for false teachers and for protection on his journeys, confirming Jesus' promise, "I will be with you always" if he obeyed. Matthew 28:20.

Neither a messenger of Satan in the form of a person, nor Satan himself would have any knowledge of paradise. He is limited. I do not read anywhere in the scripture that fallen angels are permitted to take on the form of a person as heavenly angels are permitted at times. Satan is a fallen angel, already changed from a glorious body. People can, though, do satanic things when they are under his influence. Satan can so totally invade a person's mind and body that the person's appearance, thoughts and actions may be altered and he wants to do evil continually.

2 Corinthians 11:14, 15 says, "Satan masquerades as an angel of light sometimes. It is not surprising, then, if his servants masquerade as servants of righteousness; their end will be what their actions deserve."

An example of Satan's masquerade is in these words from an unsolicited religious news sheet that came in the mail, "The religious fanatics say that God created the earth. Well, in a way he did, because he works for us! We thought of this and told him to do it and he did it! Remember, God is all things to all people, God is all substance and all energy, but not intelligence."

This deceit reminds me of the deceit of Satan used with Eve in the Garden of Eden.

Another example from the same news sheet was, "We know that the earth was created by us and for us, so we know that we are greater than the earth." Satan always tries to elevate himself and boost our ego as well. Do not fall into his trap.

The thorn Paul had was given for his own good, but it was a constant trouble, so he called it a messenger of Satan. Would Satan have known what Paul's revelations were, he would have wanted to reveal them. We ask why God did not remove the thorn? Because He allowed it as He did for Job. Satan could not give Job trouble without permission, neither could he remove it. The problem was personal for Paul. His fellow workers suffered many persecutions with him, but did not seem to carry this "thorn."

God's way to save people comes through suffering. Jesus had to suffer tremendously for mankind. Paul and the apostles suffered while establishing the church for Christ Jesus. Shall we as Christians also not suffer as well as rejoice while trying to preserve the church?

2 Timothy 2:12 says, if "we suffer with Him for Christ's sake we shall also reign with Him." This is a suffering love that responds to human needs. We agonize with others in their sufferings and endure faithfully without denying Jesus. These sufferings can be many and varied, but Christ delivers the victory.

In 1 Timothy 5:22, 23, Paul charges Timothy in duties toward different people. "Do not be hasty in the laying on of hands and do not share in the sins of others. Keep yourself pure. Stop drinking only water and use a little wine because of your stomach and your frequent illnesses." Paul prescribed some medicine here for a continuing health problem. He also said to be careful in choosing workers for the ministry. Do not lay hands on them to appoint them unless they have been proven. Do not use prejudice. as some may.

1 Timothy 5:10 talks about the character of a good widow. One characteristic is that she has relieved the afflicted, helped those in trouble and devoted herself to all kinds of good deeds.

2 Timothy 4:20 is an account of Paul leaving a helper, Trophimus, sick in Miletus. He was not healed.

In Philippians 2:26-30 we find Paul with Epaphroditus, his helper, who "became sick near death because of the work of Christ." He could not continue. Paul sent him home, recovered by the Lord's mercy. Epaphroditus "almost died for the work of Christ, even risking his life." Paul said, "Sorrow upon sorrow" would it have been had Epaphroditus died.

Paul remained faithful to God until his death. When he said good-bye to the elders at Ephesus in Acts 20:16-28, we see his commitment. ". . I consider my life worth nothing to me, if only I may finish the race and complete the task the Lord Jesus has given me — the task of testifying to the gospel of God's grace." Read it all for a more powerful understanding of his commitment.

When he left Timothy in 2 Timothy 4:1-8, he says, "I have fought a good fight. I have finished the race. I have kept the faith. Now there is in store for me the crown of righteousness, which the Lord, the righteous judge, will award to me on that day — and not only to me but also to all who have longed for His appearing."

I believe the example given by Paul, the Apostles, and Jesus Christ Himself indicates that every person that has been redeemed and is faithfully abiding in Christ can be counted among those who "long for His appearing" when they are well or when they are sick.

Philippians 4:19 promises, "God will supply all our needs and his grace is sufficient for us."

And the
prayer
offered in faith
will make the
sick person well.

Chapter IX

James On The Prayer Of Faith To Heal The Sick

James writes to his fellow Christian brothers. In chapter 1:2-4 he tells them, "Consider it pure joy, my brothers, whenever you face trials of many kinds, because you know that the testing of your faith develops perseverance. Perseverance must finish its work so that you may be mature and complete, not lacking anything." Sickness is certainly one of the trials.

In 5:13-16 he says, "Is any one of you in trouble? He should pray. Is anyone happy? Let him sing songs of praise. Is anyone of you sick? He should call the elders (In Biblical terms this would have meant bishops or church council members) of the church to pray over him and anoint him with oil in the name of the Lord, and the prayer offered in faith will make the sick person well: the Lord will raise him up. If he has sinned, he will be forgiven. Therefore confess your sins to each other and pray for each other so that you may be healed."

This does not say that church ordained ministers or elders are the only people who can be thought of to have a gift of faith or a gift of healing.

James recommends some consistency and order in the church instead of chaos. Some ministers may not have a special gift of healing but would certainly have faith in God if they are truly consecrated ministers of the Lord's work and Word. The special gifts of healing and other gifts may be given to other consecrated believers, for the Holy Spirit gives these gifts "just as He determines." 1 Corinthians 12:1-11. Someone may even receive a gift for a specific time and place or situation to confirm faith or give a testimony for Jesus. He may not need to exercise it, or be moved to use it at another time. As we exercise what the Spirit allows, we bring glory to God through obedience.

If an elder or minister of the church is sensitive to the people in a congregation, he would know if any person has a special gift of the Spirit that should or could be exercised. He would want to call upon such a person to use whatever gift he has. There are many gifts of the Spirit; and for healing, the Bible says, "The prayer of faith shall save the sick."

We should not misuse these gifts and boast about them. Jesus and His apostles did not flaunt their gifts and powers but exercised them for God's glory when it was right and necessary. James 5:16 says, "The prayer of a righteous man is powerful and effective." It gives an example — faith like that of Elijah, a prophet in the Old Testament. Verse 17 says, "Elijah was a man just like us. He prayed earnestly that it would not rain and it did not rain for three and one-half years. Again he prayed, and the heavens gave rain and the earth produced crops." See 1 Kings 17-18 for the Old Testament account.

In his book, *Doctrines of the Bible*, Dan Kauffman states, "When the sick who pray according to His will send for the elders of the church, and the elders, in harmony with the sick, pray in full faith that the prayer of faith shall save the sick, and the Lord shall raise him up, we have every reason to believe that God will hear the prayers, raise the sick, and glorify His name."

Yet, there is room for human error and someone may not have met the requirements and the person is not healed. It is not always in God's plan to physically heal every person. Or it may not be the right time. We want immediate replies, but time is not an enemy. We learn many things in time periods. God is too wise and good to always answer our prayers according to our wishes. He will do more and better things for us in His time period. Our needs and the needs of those around us are most important. Sometimes we wait. In verses 19 and 20, James says, "My brothers, if any one of you should wander from the truth and someone bring him back, remember this.

Whoever turns a sinner away from his error will save him from death and cover a multitude of sins.'' This is actually the thrust of Chapter 5 — to bring someone to Jesus and save a soul from hell.

The admonitions given before were given for the purity and strengthening of the church. When the church was established in Acts, the care of the sick appears to have been given over to the churches. The signs and miracles seem to have lessened. The message had spread and believers formed congregations, with some groups meeting in homes. The care of the sick was necessary for the good of the sick person and also the congregation. It still is necessary. It deepens members' love for each other and God, and strengthens their faith.

In Ephesians 4:11, 12 and 13 the church is defined, ''It was He who gave some to be apostles, some to be prophets, some to be evangelists and some to be pastors and teachers — to prepare God's people for works of service so that the body of Christ may be built up — until we all reach unity in the faith and in the knowledge of the Son of God and become mature, attaining to the whole measure of the fullness of Christ.''

God wants us to keep on growing so we do mature. We should not be satisfied with only 'milk' as babies get when they are born, but crave 'meat' from the word. We need not crave signs and wonders all the time. This does not say He will not allow special signs at times. We do have miracles and signs of the Spirit at various times, especially when God's word is new or not understood very well. Or when a child of His is in great danger or needs comforting, protection or healing.

A miracle is a happening above and beyond what is natural for man to do, but is normal for God. Man needs to have faith that God's word is truth, and need not be looking and asking for extra special signs. When God does allow some, it is always to confirm faith or the word that Jesus is Lord, our redeemer and friend. We have the whole universe, the church, the Bible, and the indwelling Spirit as constant signs of Jesus who Himself is a miracle to us.

Whenever a church congregation meets to worship, prayer is offered for the sick and suffering ones. At least it would be a good thing to do. I am glad to be associated with such a group of caring believers. When I was confined, it was a great comfort to me and my family to know that the church was praying for us.

Congregational support is so helpful and so necessary for its own faith and growth, and the faith and growth of the sick and suffering ones. Obedience for the whole group is important. It has a purifying effect. When one suffers, all suffer; when one rejoices, all rejoice. 1 Corinthians 12:26.

James 5:16 says, "Sins should be confessed." He could be recommending a counseling session wtih a confessing of sins for all involved, not just for 'this time' but a confessing of sin to keep us ready for any healing — a continual healing. Psalm 66:18 says, "If I regard (keep or enjoy) iniquity (sin) in my heart, He will not hear (or listen)."

It is sad when professing Chrisitan ministers do not teach nor practice this part of God's love and mercy. It has come to light in recent years that some did not even know the teaching on healing existed. Could it be that the church at large (worldwide) has been so lax in it and this is why the extremists, the sects, the cults and so-called fringe groups practice healing and almost make a God out of it and a requisite for salvation, stirring up confusion? Is this a judgment against the church for failing to be obedient, for denying a child of His this right and privilege of being healed?

When some groups practice healing, perhaps in a different way, maybe because of the Spirit's direction or just to be different or obstinate about traditions, it gives believers no right or reason to stop observing what is Biblical instruction and a privilege for a believer. To those who say, "Maybe we should not do this anymore or people will think we belong to that 'wild group,' " perhaps the words of Jesus are best, "What is that to thee? Follow thou me." This applies to all teaching, for we must read the word of God carefully and prayerfully. "Follow thou me!" Jesus said.

Looking into some background of James 5, we find that the custom in Jewish communities was for the sick to call for the elders to visit and pray for them. The early Christians considered this teaching more than a custom. It was more of a command and a privilege.

It is not a tradition. Healing could not be a tradition. Sickness could not be a tradition. Tradition said all sickness came because a person sinned. It was learned through Jesus that this was not true. Sickness comes upon us through the sin of our first parents, Adam and Eve; people now are born into a world where sin and sickness exist. Man has chosen to live contrary to God. We affect each other in this 'choice' world of greed and competition. Because of this we have personal and world ills. Sometimes there is evidence that someone is sick because of sin in his life. Gehazi's leprosy was evidence of his sin.

Sometimes we may contribute to an illness. We may hold a grudge or keep ill feelings toward others because we believe they did us an injustice once upon a time. An unforgiving spirit can fester like a sore and make us sick. Fighting conviction can make us ill. Vengeance and guilt are corrosive to the mind and body. Clouds of emotions, hate, anger, anxiety, depression, feeling inferior or superior, the complex function of memories, can all contribute to our illnesses.

Where is God when we hurt? Where is He when we have physical or emotional pain. He waits for us to communicate with him. He knows and cares.

A clear conscience lets us face all people with honesty, joy, interest and a witness to the One who forgives. The mourning of repentance brings release and comfort. Matthew 5:4.

Do we correctly label this binding, unforgiving attitude as sin? We must examine ourselves first to learn if we might have sin that we could be cultivating.

Oh no! It couldn't be me!

Sometimes it is evident, but we cannot point a finger and say "I know why!" Sad to say, though, we carry on at times as if we think we are God. We seem to believe we have all the answers to every problem and the cause for everything good that happens. We assume no responsibility for the bad.

James 5 says, "If he has committed sins, they shall be forgiven him." The person will have had confessed any sin and made certain of right relationships with those with whom there was a grievance. This is difficult with friends and family, but necessary. When the prayer of faith is offered, it shall save the sick. It had to do with us and God. He is the healer! We are the confessors.

The oil in an anointed healing is used symbolically. When priests or kings were appointed they were anointed. David says, "Thou anointest my head with oil," as an expression of joy and peace.

In ancient times oil was used as a healing compound in wounds. For example, in the story of the good Samaritan in Luke 10:34 the wounded man was oiled and bandaged by the Samaritan. Saliva was used at times, too.

This background information and instruction for healing tells us to use faith, prayer, and natural healing oil symbolic of the healing through the Spirit, His pouring out love and our confidence in God.

It suggests that medical help may also be used. People sometimes refuse treatment from medical persons. If their conscience is sensitive about this, we cannot judge them. Perhaps through false representation they do not know the full extent of God's love and mercy and do err in judgment and even in their desire for good. God and nature work in harmony, and the remedies available are made from God's supplies. These are God's provisions for a people He cares for.

The best way is always to see God first. At times we need medicine and it helps. We thank God for medicine and men that have minds able to administer and even formulate medicines, vaccines, antibiotics, cough syrups, and much more, surgery included. This is also God's provision. The drugs and medicines only become dangerous when misused.

Dr. J. G. Yoder believes that, "medicine and the practice of using it is a part of what God commands in Genesis 1:28, "Be fruitful and multiply and fill the earth and subdue it." Medicine would be part of this, controlling things that get out of control. He says further, "If sickness and suffering and decay are inherent in the creation, what can poor mortals do? Shall we sit down idly and say I am beginning to decay, so let me alone to suffer and be miserable?" That would be sad, but amusing. No, God's will is for man to live and love and help each other. He gave us minds to use and expand in knowledge that would honor Him.

Both medicine and prayer are privileges from God. We need to have a balance in the natural and He will support us with the supernatural. God works supernaturally through the natural because we understand it better that way. This is why Jesus used signs that affected human needs to help the skeptics understand that the promised Messiah had come.

Jesus was sad when He said to the skeptics, "Unless you people see miraculous signs and wonders, you will never believe." John 4:48.

In Matthew 12:38 and 16:4 and Mark 8:11, some of the Pharisees said, "Teacher, we want to see a miraculous sign from you." Jesus replied, "A wicked and adulterous generation asks for a miraculous sign! But none will be given it (generation) except the sign of the prophet Jonah. For as Jonah was three days and three nights in the belly of a huge fish, so the Son of man will be three days and three nights in the heart of the earth." He continues to say what the end will be for those who do not repent and believe in Him — death without mercy. He was the Son of God and Son of man in the flesh, and, although He gave evidence of this, they chose to not believe.

In Luke 16:31 in the story of Lazarus the beggar, Jesus said, "If they do not listen to Moses and the prophets, they will not be convinced even if someone rises from the dead."

Unbelief existed then and, for many, now too. However, we have proof beyond all the signs given to the people while Jesus was with them in person. We now have the written records and the joy of His living presence through the Holy Spirit in our hearts. What a marvelous provision!

Chapter X
Healing In The Atonement

Healing in the atonement is debated by many people.

A specific reference which points to this healing is in Isaiah 53:3-5. "Jesus was despised and rejected by men, a man of sorrows, and familiar with suffering. Like one from whom men hide their faces He was despised, and we esteemed (respected) Him not. Surely He took up our infirmities and carried our sorrows, yet we considered Him stricken by God, and smitten by Him and afflicted. But He was pierced for our transgressions, He was crushed for our iniquities; the punishment that brought us peace was upon Him, and by His stripes (wounds) we are healed (redeemed from the curse of the law which was death without mercy)."

Matthew 8:16 says, "When the evening came, many who were demon-possessed were brought to Him, and He drove out the spirits with a word and healed all the sick. This was to fulfill what was spoken through the prophet Isaiah. He took up our infirmities and carried our diseases."

Adam Clarke's *Commentary* says this refers to the taking away of sin. As diseases of the body are the emblems of the sin of the soul. Matthew refers to this prediction of Isaiah, considered the miraculous healing of the body as an emblem of the soul's salvation by Christ Jesus.

In 1 Peter 2:24 we read, He Himself bore our sins in His body on the tree, so that we might die to sins and live for righteousness; by His wounds you have been healed."

These are touching scriptures, especially when we realize it was done for us. If there had been no other person, Jesus would have been willing to die for only me. But he died for all the human race! Jesus understood that His suffering was also for the glory of the Father's will in the redemption of a fallen and rebellious race. It was an expression of His love to a hurting world. By his obedience to the Father, He brings healing to the torn and restless peoples of the world and glory to the Lord. We have limited understanding of such love, so we need to trust One who knows.

God made a way, beginning with Adam and Eve and a continuing ancestry, to let love flow through. The atonement by Jesus was meant for all people before Him and after Him.

"Salvation is like a check; God in His grace cashed the check before Jesus made the deposit which made the check good," writes J. C. Wenger in *Introduction to Theology*. Salvation is retroactive. According to Hebrews 10, the old law of sacrificing bulls and goats for the blood was not good enough. It was only symbolic of the blood of Jesus and fulfilled by Him on the cross. Matthew 1:21 says, "He will save his people from their sins." The law in the Old Testament was given to prepare people to see their need of a Saviour, to learn right from wrong, and to teach God's holiness. In the New Testament the Saviour came to us in the flesh.

The dictionary says atonement means a satisfactory reparation for an offense or injury; a satisfactory reconciliation. The redeeming effect of Christ's sacrifice on the cross. A reconciliation between God and people. This is spiritual, but it also affects us emotionally, mentally and physically:

1. Restores holiness — if we commit our lives totally to Him.

2. Mentally — we will to do His will.

3. Emotionally — guilt and fear are removed, we have peace.

4. Physically — although naturally decaying, we are preserved to work and live happily where He wills.

There is a relationship, though, between the atonement and the healing of the body.

2 Corinthians 4:16 says, "The inner person is being renewed day by day by the Spirit of God dwelling within."

God in His wisdom saw the need for touching. A newborn baby grows better when it is touched by someone who loves it, according to the book, *Fearfully and Wonderfully Made* by Dr. Paul Brand and Philip Yancey. This has also been proven by the experiences of others.

In the same way, God provided this special personal ministry of touching through the Spirit. He set in motion a Christian mission for us to also reach out and touch others. The atonement is an obedient, loving, forgiving, total healing sacrifice.

The physical outer person is wasting away and will only be completely renewed when he is changed into His likeness. This can only come by death and resurrection.

Though our sins have been atoned for, we must wait for the full effects of salvation until our own resurrection. Romans 8:22, 23 says, "We know that the whole creation has been groaning as in the pains of childbirth right up to the present time. Not only so, but we ourselves, who have the first fruits of the Spirit, groan inwardly as we wait eagerly for our adoption as sons, the redemption of our bodies." Verse 26 continues, "In the same way, the Spirit helps us in our weaknesses (infirmities). We do not know what we ought to pray, but the Spirit himself intercedes for us with groans that words cannot express."

This plainly states that our salvation and redemption process will only be complete when our sins are remitted at the resurrection.

If, in the atonement, a person believes salvation is complete because Jesus bore our sins, then he must also believe Jesus bore death completely and we will not die anymore. If physical healing would be only in the atonement, only the saints or saved could be healed. The records show that Jesus healed some who did not believe in Him as the Son of God. Also, if total healing is in the atonement only, by praying we should always receive. Paul did not always receive as he desired. Neither did some others. Jesus does say, "Ask and receive," but ask according to His will.

2 Corinthians 5:21 says, "God made Him who had no sin to be sin for us so that in Him we might become the righteousness of God." Jesus took away the curse of the law, death

without mercy. "With his stripes we are healed." We now have 'death with mercy,' but the sting of death without mercy remains in the natural man.

The sting of death is sin and the power of sin is the law. "But thanks be to God! He gives us the victory through our Lord Jesus Christ," 1 Corinthians 15:56.

Instead of sickness being a curse, we have sufferings without condemnation. We continue to bear the susceptibility to sickness. As we are in the process of being repossessed spiritually and still have a natural body, not a glorified body, we are subject to decay and death. The "new creatures" we have become as believers are not alone anymore. The Spirit helps us to be victorious through and over sickness.

A person does not normally will to get sick, but he does will to sin. God does not will for someone to sin or be sick, because He wills only good for His children. God does permit both evil and sickness. It is not a sin to be sick and not a sin to be well all the time. Because of our nature, God allows some sin and certain results of sin and adversity including sickness, to execute His plan of love, mercy and justice.

Ephesians 2:3 says, 'We were by nature objects of wrath." Unregenerate, we are in the world because one of us chose to anger God in Eden. We have a nature, if left alone, would be displeasing to God, but by choosing Jesus Christ as our Redeemer we have been given a new nature. We are regenerated. We have been 'regened.' We have been generated by the Spirit of God. Instead of our flesh first, we choose to put Christ and His work first.

In Ephesians 3:10, 11, Paul speaks to the Gentiles, "God's intent was that now through the church (people with a new nature) the manifold wisdom of God should be made known . . . according to his eternal purpose which he accomplished in Christ Jesus. In him and through faith in him we may approach God with freedom and confidence."

Freely we can come to God for He is our Father. We can ask for forgiveness of sins and healing for the sick body, our hidden sick attitudes, sick thoughts, sickly lustful ideas, dirty scheming minds and more. It is easy in this age of television and pornography to fill our minds with unhealthy thoughts. How often this is done! We can ask for victory over these sins and the guilt and condemnation they bring. As children of God, we can trust His judgment as he cares for us. We receive what is best for us and those around us. Always in love. Always for better, never worse. Psalm 103:13, 14 says, "As a father his compassion on his children, so the Lord has compassion on those that fear Him."

Again the compassion of the Father is shown in verse 14, "For he knows how we are formed, he remembers that we are dust."

Matthew 7:11 speaks about the compassion of the Father. God is very gracious concerning His children. We can believe it and claim it when we are well or when we are sick, all because of His atoning work of love on the cross. Read all of Psalm 103.

May every child of God and every unbeliever seek to understand what the Bible teaches about the greatness of the grace of God. Through His love and grace alone has there been made an atonement for sinful people, giving to each one an assurance of salvation and hope for eternity.

We can be at peace with such a gracious Lord. "Praise the Lord, O my soul; all my inmost being, praise his holy name." Psalm 103:1

"As long as the earth remains,
seedtime and harvest,
cold and heat,
summer and winter,
day and night,
will never cease."

One of the many promises of God we believe by
faith.

We expect to see the sunrise on the morrow
We believe that God put a rainbow in the sky
When we are sure that somewhere love is living
Then faith has taken root to occupy.

LB

Chapter XI

Faith Defined — Hebrews 11:1

The New International Version — "Now faith is being sure of what we hope for, and certain of what we do not see."
The King James Version — "Now faith is the substance of things hoped for, the evidence of things not seen."

FAITH IS

  believing

    may or may not imply certainty or evidence

 always believes even without evidence

 Biblical faith rests upon the revealed Word of God

THE SUBSTANCE

   unchanging position without evidence

  foundation on which to build

   the solid material of which it is made

OF THINGS HOPED FOR

    an expectant trusting

  looking ahead for blessings in the heart

    unseen but hopeful; hope is for good

  future life, peace, resurrection — to see Jesus

THE EVIDENCE

  proof   demonstration of both

  certainty   no doubt; cannot be otherwise

OF THINGS NOT SEEN

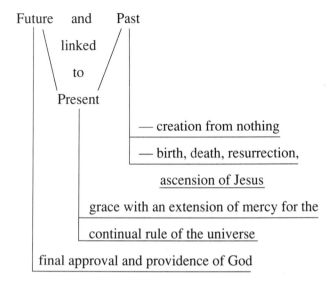

"For in this hope we were saved. But hope that is seen is not hope at all. Who hopes for what he already has? But we hope for what we do not yet have, we wait patiently for it." Romans 8:14-25.

Faith

"Faith comes from hearing the message, and the message is heard through the word of Christ." Romans 10:17.

By using one of our five senses, the ears, we hear; then we receive.

Ephesians 2:8 — "For it is by grace you have been saved, through faith — and this is not of yourselves, it is the gift of God." It is a saving faith given freely by God after we hear.

Hebrews 11:1-3 — "Now faith is being sure of what we hope for and certain of what we do not see. This is what the ancients were commended for.

"By faith we understand that the universe was formed at God's command so that what is seen was not made out of what was visible."

Hebrews 11:6 — "Without faith, it is impossible to please God." God limits Himself to respond to our faith. How much do we want to please God? The more we want to please, the more our faith increases.

2 Corinthians 5:7 — "We live by faith and not by sight." This is the spiritual faith which all and only Christians have. It is the kind of faith we have that believes God's promises and His ability to keep them. We sin if we do not have faith in what the Word says. "Whatsoever is not of faith is sin." Romans 14:23

2 Corinthians 12:9 — This faith is a gift of the Holy Spirit. It is a special gift of faith. George Mueller, a missionary of great faith and prayer, seems to have had a special gift of faith. He prayed for and received millions of dollars to help orphaned children. He claims he just exercised what he had. What a source of power is true faith for a believer! Anyone has the privilege of exercising the gift of spiritual faith.

John 14:1-14 — Faith in Christ brings power for service to do greater things. The known world at the time of Christ was not as large as we know it. Now, we can witness to the uttermost parts of the earth. Many more people can be converted to Christ. Miraculous works of the Spirit of God are proofs of God's mighty power.

John 10:37, 38 — "Believe the evidence of miracles as proof of the relationship between the Son and the Father." During the earthly ministry of Jesus, he gave much evidence of this relationship.

John 11:40 — Jesus says, "Did I not tell you, if you believed, you would see the glory of God?"

Mark 11:22-26 — Have strong faith in God. Forgive and be forgiven. When we have an unforgiving attitude it is a hindrance to faith and prayer. It can sedate a growing faith. We want to cultivate faith to become a strong, courageous person for the Lord.

Matthew 23:23 — Jesus lists faith as one of the important matters of the law, just like justice and mercy, and chastises the teachers of the law for neglecting them. He points out the hypocrisy of following the letter of the law by tithing while neglecting faith, mercy and justice.

James 2:14-26 — Faith without works is dead. A person could perhaps be a professing Christian, but not be enjoying a fruitful spirit-filled life. This would grieve the Spirit. Because he has not surrendered every area of his life to Jesus through faith, there can be no joy nor fruitfulness.

Galatians 5:6 — Faith is a fruit of the Spirit expressed through love. It is very worthwhile to have this fruit.

John 20:26-29 — Thomas needed proof of Jesus' resurrection, so Jesus showed him His nail scars and said to him, "Because you have seen me, you have believed; blessed are those who have not seen and yet have believed."

Faith is by choice. Spiritual faith is accepting God as a real personality. Accepting His Word as truth. Accepting God as an experience.

"When we are called to follow Christ, we are summoned to an exclusive attachment to His person," wrote Dietrich Bonhoeffer in *The Cost of Discipleship*.

First comes faith, then experience, then increased faith. Faith is the first step for anyone wanting to please God. Spiritual faith is based and rests on the revealed Word of God. It is trust without reservation and is not blind nor unreasoning. You can have no spiritual faith outside the known will of God. To exercise it is to increase it.

Matthew 6:33 — "But seek first his kingdom and his righteousness and all these (good) things will be given to you as well."

Sometimes God may set us apart for unexpected special tasks so that His will can be fulfilled. This, of course, would take an act of faith to follow His leading.

Faith is acting. Read Hebrews 11. It discusses how by faith people served for righteousness sake. Through faith we can expect growth and blessing, but need to distinguish between faith or only feeling good about something we have done, because certain feelings may be deceitful and have nothing to do with faith in God.

Certain teachings of "truth and light" from some religious fringe groups, cults, gurus or transcendentalists may make a person feel good but have nothing to do with spiritual faith. Satan may be presented as an angel of light who goes about with subtlety and deceit to gloss it over. No spiritual faith is involved in the disguised enticement.

Luke 17:5 — The apostles said to Christ, "Increase our faith." So also must we say, "Increase our faith."

Romans 1:17 — "For in the gospel a righteousness from God is revealed, a righteousness that is by faith from first to last, just as it is written, 'The righteous will live by faith.' "

Habakkuk 2:4 — "The just shall live by faith." (KJV) It means the same, that faith is an ongoing necessity for a righteous person.

Romans 5:1-11 — "Therefore, since we have been justified through faith, we have peace with God through our Lord Jesus Christ." Justified means just as if it had not been, that we had not sinned. Read to verse 11.

Spiritual faith is a strong belief in God as a living presence within us and a governing presence over us and all His creation. A belief that is sure and trustworthy. This knowledge is a big help when we are well or sick or have other adversities. When we know and believe that the Lord can heal, would it not be a denial of our faith in Him to complain and get angry, or oppose Him? Read Acts 11:17. ". . . who was I to think that I could oppose God?"

1 John 5:4 — "For everyone born of God has overcome the world. This is the victory that has overcome the world, even our faith." It is by faith we can look beyond to the things that are invisible. We walk by faith and not by sight, by trusting our Guide and Counselor, having hope through Jesus Christ.

A believer never hopes for what is bad. He expects good things by faith. By faith we understand that God gives His children good things.

Spiritual faith belongs to the Christian only. God gives a person power to believe, then the person acts on his own. To just believe God and not act is like a well without water. We cannot go through life without faith. "Without faith it is impossible to please God," Hebrews 11:6.

Faith is orderly — as God is.

We hear . . . we receive . . . we act . . . we exercise by obedience . . . we obey because we love . . . we love because we have forgiveness of sins . . . we have forgiveness of sins because we ask . . . we ask because we recognize sin . . . we sin because we are of Adam's human race. Jesus was divine and human, yet without sin. Believers take on some divine qualities which identify them as spiritually-minded.

One mark of faith is divine love. This love goes beyond normal expectations. It loves the lovely and the unlovely. It bears the bearable and the unbearable. It looks for the good instead of evil.

Faith is positive, but it is more than just a positive attitude. We could relax in our easy chairs, lie in sick beds, busy ourselves and say, "Think positive. All is well .. I've got it." Such faith is dead. Faith needs exercise, then it grows. It gives life balance.

Faith works.

Faith cares.

Faith believes.

Faith is not easily attracted to worldly pleasures nor swayed by every wind of doctrine that blows. It is marked by hope, obedience, peace, prayerfulness, power, patience, assurance of the word, eternal values, steadfastness and joyfulness. The Word of God says if we are faithful, we will have adversities.

Acts 14:22 — The disciples preached the good news of salvation and also were strengthened by other disciples. They encouraged each other to remain true to the faith. " 'We must go through many hardships to enter the kingdom of God,' they said."

131

John 16:33 — Jesus said, "I have told you these things, so that in me you may have peace. In this world you will have trouble. But take heart! I have overcome the world."

1 Peter 5:10 — "And the God of all grace, who called you to his eternal glory in Christ, after you have suffered a little while, will himself restore you and make you strong, firm and steadfast."

We are promised hardship and suffering.

Where then is joy?

Joy comes from believing that God promises victory over adversities, that through adversities God's name can be magnified and His cause furthered. A Christian believer does not overcome "just somehow," but triumphantly, victoriously and joyfully with love and obedience to God. This is joy the world without spiritual faith does not and cannot know, for that world does not understand God's love. Neither can a Christian expect that world to understand.

Total submission is another mark of faith. Jesus expressed total submission when He said, "Thy will be done," to his heavenly Father, even though He already knew it was God's will. This total submission was expressed at a crucial time in His humanity. He was not yet glorified, but ready to be crucified.

Amazing things happen when we totally commit our lives into God's care and keeping.

A past president of Columbia Bible College said for Christians to dare to be "utterly believing believers." He further challenged Christians and churches with "no fire" or with "wild fire" to seek the "heavenly fire (Holy Spirit) without the fanaticism of the flesh." (*Crowded to Christ* by L. E. Maxwell).

This would be honoring God and inspiring people to move by faith. At whatever angle we view life or whatever age we are in, we need to grow through a maturing process in order to become further conformed to the image of God's Son.

Faith in God's Word helps establish us.

Faith in God keeps us.

Faith Is a Living Power from Heaven

246

We are . . . of them that believe to the saving of the soul.—HEB. 10: 39

P. HERBERT, 1566   SESSIONS L. M.   L. O. EMERSON, 1847

1. Faith is a liv-ing pow'r from heav'n Which grasps the
2. Faith finds in Christ what-e'er we need To save and
3. Faith to the con-science whis-pers peace; And bids the
4. Such faith in us, O God, im-plant, And to our

prom - ise God has giv'n; Se - cure-ly fixed on
strength-en, guide and feed; Strong in His grace it
mourn-er's sigh-ing cease; By faith the chil-dren's
prayers Thy fa - vor grant, In Je - sus Christ, Thy

Christ a - lone, A trust that can - - not be o'er-thrown.
joys to share His cross, in hope...... His crown to wear.
right we claim, And call up - on........ our Fa - ther's name.
sav - ing Son, Who is our fount..... of health a - lone.

133

To talk with God
No breath is lost....
Talk on!

To walk with God
No strength is lost....
Walk on!

To wait on God
No time is lost...
Talk on!

Chapter XII
Prayer

Prayer is — talking with God.

— a conscious fellowship with God.

— the expression of oneself to God.

A little Scottish lad told the great minister of the Gospel, D. L. Moody the following words for a definition of prayer. "Prayer is an offering up of our desires unto God for things agreeable to His will, in the name of Christ, with confession of our sins and thankful acknowledgement of His mercies."

This lad had it memorized correctly. It is difficult, though, to prescribe exactly for another person how to pray for definite things, because needs differ. It may be easy to talk and write about praying, but to practice praying in the Spirit and unto God could be very hard.

These thoughts and guidelines may be helpful.

Prayer is — Worship and adoration. Beginning and ending with God and who he really is. He is an eternal, invisible, almighty God who created the worlds and everything in them. He is our heavenly Father. He wants us to come into His presence with mind and heart. So often our mind is thinking about what we want or need that it wanders. We give very little thought to God himself. We must consciously come to God when we pray.

Prayer is — a privilege for the Christian. It is not and never should be just a religious activity. It should not become a mechanical routine habit. If it does, prayer will be powerless and ineffective.

Prayer is — the only way a sinner has to confess his sin and receive forgiveness for them. It is an indispensable, vital work.

Prayer is — asking. In John 16:24, Jesus told His disciples, "Until now you have not asked for anything in my name. Ask and you will receive and your joy will be complete."

This sounds like Exodus 6:3 when God and Moses were talking about plans for the exodus of the children of Israel from Egypt. God said, "I am the Lord, I appeared to Abraham, to Isaac and to Jacob as God Almighty (all sufficient and with power to do good). But by my name Jehovah (Lord) I did not make myself known."

In Psalm 83:18 David said, "Let them know that you, whose name is the LORD, that you alone are the Most High over all the earth."

Lord signifies existence. Now, by confirming His name, God gave life or meaning to the promises He had already made. Jesus reminded the disciples, "I told you, now just ask. You have not done that yet. I will do as I promised."

Matthew 7:7 — "Ask and it shall be given you, seek and you shall find, knock and it shall be opened up to you."

1 Kings 3:5 — God told Solomon, "Ask for whatever you want me to give you." Solomon asked for wisdom and God gave it to him. He also gave Solomon riches and honor as an added blessing.

James 1:5-8 — "If any of you lack wisdom, he should ask of God, who gives generously to all without finding fault, and it will be given to him. But when he asks, he must believe, (have faith) and not doubt, because he who doubts is like a wave of the sea, blown and tossed by the wind. That man should not think he will receive anything from the Lord; he is a double-minded man unstable in all he does." Doubts are seeds of unbelief, but honest prayer can keep them from sprouting and growing.

Prayer is — communciation on the highest level known to man. Matthew 6:11 — "Give us this day our daily bread." Simple, humble but eloquent. It concerns our daily needs. Philippians 4:6-7 — "Do not be anxious about anything, but in everything by prayer and petition with thanksgiving, present your requests to God. And the peace of God which transcends all understanding will guard your hearts and minds in Christ Jesus." This is marvelous and lofty!

Prayer is — thanksgiving and petition. Ingratitude is sin. Romans 1:21

Prayer is — commanded. Luke 18:1 — "Men ought always to pray." 1 Timothy 2:8 — "I will therefore that men pray everywhere lifting up holy hands without anger or disputing." It is God's will. "Pray without ceasing." 1 Thessalonians 5:17. Have a right attitude. Live in the spirit of prayer. Be God conscious.

Prayer is — having a sense of God's living presence within. In Psalm 25:1, David wrote, "Unto thee, O Lord, do I lift up my soul." He offered his innermost being.

Prayer is — a means of receiving the Holy Spirit in our lives. Acts 1:14 and Acts 2:1-4 tell about the first appearance of the Spirit after Jesus ascended to heaven. Acts 4:31 says prayer gives power to testify because of the Holy Spirit.

Prayer is — the only way to know God's continuing will for us. Psalm 50:23 — "He who sacrifices thank offerings honors me, and he prepares the way so that I may show him the salvation of God." John 15:7 — "If you remain in me and my words remain in you, ask whatever you wish, and it will be done for you." 1 John 5:14, 15 — "This is the assurance we have in approaching God; that if we ask anything according to his will he hears us. And if we know that he hears us, whatever we ask, we know that we have what we asked of him."

The purposes of God are being fulfilled through prayer. God moves behind the scenes so we must leave the results of prayer to Him. It requires our faithfulness but the results are God's responsibility. 1 Samuel 12:23 describes Samuel's outstanding attitude toward sinful Israel, "As for me, God forbid that I should sin against the Lord in ceasing to pray for you." In Ezekiel 22:30 is a profoundly moving message. Because Israel had sinned, God said, "I looked for a man among them who would build up the wall and stand in the gap on behalf of the land, so I would not destroy it, but I found none." It was a missed opportunity.

Prayer is — confession. When we sense our own sinfulness and helplessness, we confess it to God. Confessing our sin is really agreeing with God in His judgment of the sin, its guilt and seriousness. We give it to Him. We need to acknowledge Him in our confessions. We also need to acknowledge our individual acts. Forgiveness is available.

Prayer is — the support necessary for obeying God. 1 John 3:21-24 — "Dear friends, if our hearts do not condemn us, we have confidence before God and receive from him anything we ask because we obey his commands and do what pleases him. And this is his command; to believe . . . love . . . obey . . ." In Luke 6:47, 48 we see an example of support. Jesus reminds us that a house built on sand could collapse, but one built on rock is firm and will last. A good foundation is most important for a believer. We need some support to build on.

Prayer is — protection against Satan and his works. It is the most secret weapon we have. Matthew 26:41 — "Watch and pray so that you will not fall into temptation. The spirit is willing, but the body is weak."

Prayer is — the most private and secret blessing we have. It allows us to talk about something no one else can know unless we so desire. Just God and I. Matthew 6:5-15 — Jesus emphasized secret prayer, but does not exclude public prayer. I believe the Lord is pleased and honored when the church gets together to pray and worship, or when small groups pray together. He says to guard against trying to make an impression and using vain repetitions. His instructions are: "But when you pray, do not be like the hypocrites, for they love to pray standing in the synagogues and on the street corners to be seen by men. I tell you the truth, they have received their reward in full. When you pray go to your room, close the door and pray to your Father, who is unseen. Then your Father, who sees what is done in secret, will reward you. And when you pray, do not keep on babbling like pagans, for they think they will be heard because of their many words. Do not be like them, for your Father knows what you need before you ask him. This is how you should pray:

" 'Our Father which art in heaven.
Hallowed be thy name.
Thy kingdom come,
Thy will be done
     on earth, as it is in heaven.
Give us this day our daily bread
And forgive us our debts.
     as we forgive our debtors.
And lead us not into temptation,
but deliver us from evil.'
For thine is the kingdom,
and the power, and the glory, forever. Amen.

"For if you forgive men when they sin against you your heavenly Father will also forgive you. But if you do not forgive men their sins, your Father will not forgive your sins." (6:14, 15)

These are awesome words!

The Lord's Prayer is given as a model prayer, or a pattern to follow. It is not necesary to repeat it at every meeting or other prayer times. It could become a meaningless, vain repetition. The total meaning is important. We pray unto God and empty ourselves so he can fill us. Forgiveness is very critical or we cannot receive forgiveness ourselves. In Matthew 18:20-21 Peter asked Jesus, "Lord, how many times shall I forgive my brother when he sins against me? Up to seven times? Jesus answered, 'I tell you, not seven times but seventy-seven times.' " Then Jesus told a parable about an unmerciful servant.

Nothing in life will do more or be better in giving us joy and contentment than prayer. It also gives strength, peace and confidence. Especially when we are tested with an illness.

A good way to get started in a personal prayer life anytime, is to read the scriptures and let them speak to you. Find yourself asking for wisdom and understanding. Talk to God about the things you read and how it fits in His plans for you.

We must be humble enough to receive from God's word what he wants to enable us to receive. We are not always ready to receive some enlightenment. But God has worked that out well, because the Spirit knows if we are not ready, and when we are ready, He will inform us. At times we need to wait for more understanding or light.

We should not make the Bible an end in itself. John 5:39-40 — "You diligently study the scriptures because you think that by them you possess eternal life. These are the scriptures that testify of me, yet you refuse to come to me to have life." We can, but need not become trapped by just knowing much of what the scriptures say and feel smug and satisfied with ourselves. The scriptures teach that Jesus is life. We must learn through the Word, but need to focus on the person of Jesus Christ. Our life depends on Him!

Prayer is — an unlimited power, not given as a burden to be carried. Hebrews 4:16 — "Let us approach the throne of grace with confidence, so that we may receive mercy and find grace to help us in our time of need." Power and mercy never quit. We find that people of power are people of prayer. People were created for continuous fellowship with God. Through prayer we can fulfill this purpose, even to our subconscious mind. Sometimes a certain fear or shadow of an unpleasant memory hiding in the subconscious mind can be a hindrance to the fellowship with God. But He is the power from which we receive a release from these distressing problems. God's attention is on us continually, but he wants us to tell him our needs for the relationship it brings between us and Him.

Matthew 6:8 — "He knows what we need before we ask." The function of prayer is to put God at the center of our attention. Matthew 6:33 — "Seek first his kingdom and his righteousness, and all these things (good) will be given to you as well."

Prayer is — receiving or getting an answer from God in God's time. Yes, no, or wait, but always answered. If the answer to a prayer seems like a "No" to us and through prayer we become a better person, the answer is positive and becomes "Yes." A seeming denial to a request should be understood as God's protection and not a punishment.

James 4:2, 3 — "You do not have because you do not ask. When you do not ask you do not receive, because you ask with wrong motives, that you may spend what you get on your pleasures." Any unconfessed sin or wrongdoing is a hindrance to prayer.

Broken relationships between other people or between husbands and wives are hindrances to effective prayer. The relationship to God cannot be right when the fellowship with others is gone. Anger, lust, envy, pride, gossip or whatever else becomes a barrier between people is also a barrier between us and God.

1 John 1:6-7 — "If we claim to have fellowship with Him yet walk in the darkness, we lie and do not live by the truth. But if we walk in the light, as he is in the light, we have fellowship with one another, and the blood of Jesus, His Son, purifies us from all sin." The reason I mention relationships so strongly is that broken ones often cause a depression or can cause an illness for some people. If so, the problem existed before the break. Confession and healing must take place to restore the right relationships.

Do we limit God in making requests? Do we ask sometimes in all sincerity for something we want very much, even something good for us, but do not do our part in getting the reply? So how can God give it? We must make the condition right.

Perhaps we pray for the things that feed the flesh only. Perhaps we try a compromise or demand something selfishly. Romans 7:18 says, "I know that nothing good lives in me, that is, in my sinful nature. For I have the desire to do what is good, but I cannot carry it out." Paul talks here about struggling with sin. Either a well person or a sick person faces this sin problem.

We want to ask with the right motives and expect an answer. We want to be willing to have God have His way with us. We want to strive to have His will be done.

When we pray for some person to be saved, we know it is God's will, no doubt. 2 Peter 3:9 specifies, "He is not willing that any should perish, but that all should come to repentance."

1 Timothy 2:4 also says, "Who will have all men to be saved and to come to the knowledge of the truth."

We just must say, "Your will be done." Submission is allowing God to have His way with us.

John 3:16 — "For God so loved the world that he gave his one and only Son, that whoever believes on him shall not perish but have everlasting life."

Matthew 7:7-12 — ". . . What man is there of you whom if his son asks bread will give him a stone? Or if he asks for a fish will give him a snake? . . ." We can expect good answers when we ask for ourselves or others according to His will. The Holy Spirit helps us. This is why He was sent to us, because we sometimes don't know how to ask. But Jesus says, "Ask," and promises, "Receive."

It is right! Never be too busy to pray! When God walks with us we can even breathe a prayer. He hears. Praise God for the privilege of prayer. Always be thankful. "By prayer and supplication (petition) with thanksgiving, present your requests to God."

Prayer is — God the Holy Spirit speaking to God the Father in the name of God the Son, "and the believer's heart is the prayer room."

We pray in the name of Jesus because He is the one that paid the price for our redemption. The blood work Jesus gave on the cross was and is the legal and sacrificial purchase price for our soul's salvation, our forgiveness of sin. It satisfied God. Hebrews 10:19 — "We have boldness to enter into the holiest by the blood of Jesus." It was paid in advance. If we do not believe in the atonement for sin, we cannot pray in the name of Jesus. To pray in His name is to pray as a representative of His. He gave us His name to use. He made a commitment to us by His spirit and His will.

Keep in mind the need to glorify the Father. Jesus has given us His name to use. How careful we must be that our lives are lived to be worthy of that name. When we have a legal document to sign we are very careful to put the right signature on it, especially where money is involved. Jesus counted

143

His children worthy to use His name. Humbly we say, "Lord, teach us to pray."

It is not required to use fancy words to pray. He knows our needs. When we pray in His name we ask for things He has bought for us. We cannot ask foolishly and attach "in Jesus' name," thinking it will make it a perfect prayer. We need to request the things He can endorse.

Exodus 20:7 — "Do not take the name of the Lord your God in vain (do not misuse) for the Lord will not hold him guiltless that takes His name in vain." How often we take His name in vain. God forgive us!

We do need to pray for special things, even small things. We do need to pray for mighty things.

We have some outstanding Biblical examples of people praying for mighty things. They were people who were faithful to God. They received answers. In Exodus 32:9-14 Moses by prayer reversed the wrath of God. I call that power! Joshua 10:12-14 says the sun and moon stood still because of prayer. In 2 Kings 1:19 Elijah called fire down from heaven, and another time, according to James 5:17, he prayed for rain to stop for three years and then begin again. In 2 Kings 2:3, 14 Elisha divided the water. Daniel's prayers in Daniel 6:10 revealed the power of God to a nation. Also, throughout the New Testament, we read about Paul's and the apostle's many experiences of power through prayer.

Jesus was and is the Son of God, and also the Son of man in the flesh and knew the need for communication with the Father in heaven. A look at His prayer life tells us some improtant times of prayer for Him.

Luke 3:20 — at His own baptism.

Mark 1:35 — in a solitary place.

Luke 5:16 — in the wilderness.

Luke 6:12 — all night before choosing the 12 disciples.

Matthew 11:25-27 — before his invitation, "Come unto me."

John 6:11 — at the feeding of the 5,000 He gave thanks for food.

Matthew 14:23 — after feeding the 5,000 He sent the multitude away and went away to pray.

Luke 11:1-4 and Matthew 6:9-13 — Lord's prayer. In a certain place.

Luke 9:18 — praying alone.

Luke 9:29 — at the transfiguration.

Matthew 19:13 — blessing little children. Not baptizing, but laying hands on them.

John 11:41, 42 — before raising Lazarus from the dead.

John 12:27, 28 — in the temple.

Matthew 26:26, 27 — at the institution of communion.

Luke 22:32 — for Peter, so that his faith would not fail.

John 17 — for Himself, disciples and others.

Matthew 26:36, 39, 42, 44 — agonizing in Gethsemane, prostrate. A prayer of submission, "Thy will be done."

Luke 23:24 — on the cross, for forgiveness for His enemies.

Luke 24:30 — at Emmaus to bless food.

Jesus was knowledgeable about the world in which He lived. He also knew of the unseen world and the forces and powers that are veiled to us. We cannot sometimes understand or explain the full intended meaning of some thought in the scriptures. Where there is a veil, we need not speculate on what is not there. As we become more learned through prayer and reading, our understanding will be opened. When the Bible is silent, we need to be silent, too.

2 Timothy 3:14-17 tells us that we should continue to be convinced of the holy scriptures. They are able to make us "wise . . . for salvation through faith in Christ Jesus . . .," when we exercise love, patience, persistence in practicing prayer, we can reach goals we thought impossible.

Again, keep in mind to glorify God. Jesus did not talk or pray just to hear Himself. His aim was always to bring glory to the Father. This should be our aim.

When we pray we should keep in mind that Jesus is our very own unseen friend. Jesus told His disciples in John 15:1-27, ". . . I no longer call you servants, because a servant does not know his master's business. Instead, I have called you friends, for everything that I learned from my Father I have made known to you . . . ." In faith we keep in mind this unseen friend and do not need to look at material objects that might become idols to us or detract in honoring the name of Jesus.

The position of a person in prayer is not important. When someone is in a prayerful frame of mind, I do not think God is concerned whether they sit, stand, bow, kneel or are prostrate. But He does say in Romans 14:11 that, "Every knee will bow before me; every tongue will confess to God."

Philippians 2:9-11 says:

> *"Therefore God exalted him to the*
> *highest place*
> *and gave him the name that is above*
> *every name,*
> *that at the name of Jesus every knee*
> *should bow,*
> *in heaven and on earth and under the*
> *earth,*
> *and every tongue confess that Jesus*
> *Christ is Lord,*
> *to the glory of God the Father."*

If we never practice bowing here, we will at another time. Bowing or kneeling is a humbling position. It is one of respect. Whatever position we take, we must always take time to pray.

The Spirit then works like a generator that takes over in a hospital when the power goes off. It brings current and the power produces energy to bring light. The Spirit is on call constantly to help whenever we ask. This is pleasing to God.

In James 5:13 we read, "Is anyone in trouble? He should pray. Is anyone happy? Let him sing songs of praise." These are definite instructions. We can do both. Prayer is a great healer and singing praises is good medicine. The Bible promises that the prayer of faith shall heal the sick. Prayer is vital to a Christian's life when he is well or sick.

In Luke 11 Jesus answered a disciple's request, "Lord, teach us to pray."

In Psalm 115:1 is a reminder of the need to glorify God. "Not to us, O Lord, not to us but to your name be the glory, because of your love and faithfulness."

I pray now with you:

"Our Father in heaven, Creator and keeper of this great universe where we live from day to day. For your sovereign works among us we praise and thank you. We thank you for allowing us to be your children. Your presence is so necessary in our lives. We need strength and courage from you each day as we face a world that works selfishly. We thank you that you know what each day holds for us. Help us to use each day for your glory. Cleanse us from anything that would hinder your work in our lives. May the good within us be magnified day by day, and our weaknesses be overcome so that our lives can be lived victoriously in any kind of circumstance. We commit ourselves into your care and keeping and ask that in the name of Jesus you will receive glory and we a blessing."

Amen. L.B.

" But such is the
irresistible nature
of truth, that all
it asks, and all it
wants, is the
liberty of
appearing. "

Thomas Paine

Chapter XIII
The Will Of God

What is the will of God?

The dictionary states that by law a will is a legal declaration of a person's mind as to the manner in which he would want his estate disposed of after his death.

I believe this is a good description of God's will, except that it would be executed while and because He is living. The eternal Holy Spirit acts as the executor. The whole created universe and we, His people, are His estate. He has given us a written document in the Word, the Bible, with instructions about how His estate should be used. How, why, when, where and to whom. The Word, the Father, his ascended Son Jesus Christ our Lord and the Holy Spirit agree.

In John 15:26 Jesus said, ". . . The Spirit of truth who goes out from the Father, he will testify about me . . ." The Spirit brings the will of God to the attention of every believer.

The will of God is simply doing what He wants us to do; what He knows is best for us. He desires good for us, not evil. Ephesians 5:15-17 says, "Be very careful, then, how you live — not as unwise but as wise, making the most of every opportunity, because the days are evil. Therefore do not be foolish, but understand what the Lord's will is."

In order to do His will, we must first be a child of His. Otherwise His will can never be revealed. Next, we must be obedient and wait on the Lord. Galatians 5:5 says, "But by faith we eagerly await through the Spirit the righteousness for which we hope." It takes faith in God to know His will.

The will of God is that people are saved from an eternal death. His desire and will is that people should have eternal life. By having faith in Jesus and His sacrifice on the cross, with a confession of sins, this is possible. The sin is forgiven. God is not "willing that any should perish." 2 Peter 3:9.

In John 6:38-40 Jesus said, "I have come down from heaven not to do my will but to do the will of him who sent me. And this is the will of him who sent me, that I shall lose none of all that he has given me, but raise them up at the last day. For my Father's will is that everyone who looks to the Son and believes in him shall have eternal life, and I will raise him up at the last day." This too, says that the will of God is for the children of God when they are sick, well, maimed, lame, blind or suffering in another way.

A closer look will tell us that the workings of the Spirit can only be discerned or understood spiritually. He will not reveal His will to a sinner. 1 Corinthians 2:14 says, "The man without the Spirit does not accept the things that come from the Spirit of God, for they are foolishness to Him and he cannot understand them, because they are spiritually discerned."

Many Christians think the will of God is a puzzle or a mystery. The Bible tells us many times what the will of God is for a believer. God has given us a full revelation of His will in the Bible. We need to understand his plan for us in that will or just accept Him and be obedient even when we do not fully understand.

God's will is to love.

In John 15:12 Jesus said, "My command is this: Love each other as I have loved you." A plain and simple command. Is it hard to love another person through the eyes of God? We make hard work out of it sometimes because we let self get in the way. Love is of God. "And I pray that you, being rooted and established in love, may have power, together with all the saints, to grasp how wide and long and high and deep is the love of Christ." Ephesians 3:17, 18.

When we think of the sacrificial love that Jesus demonstrated to the world, we should want to be obedient to the best of our ability. This will require patiently waiting on Him until we comprehend where we fit in His plans. We walk by faith. Isaiah 40:31 gives us a good Christian exercise program. It says that those who wait upon or . . . "hope in the Lord will renew their strength. They will soar on wings like eagles; they will run and not grow weary, they shall walk and not be faint."

151

God's will provides order in the life of a Christian. It is His plan to have a definite place in each person's life. This is possible through his ascended Son and the indwelling Holy Spirit. He cares about every aspect of a person's life. Read Genesis 1 and 2 and Psalm 139 which tells how very carefully He planned creation and how He is everywhere present. He has a plan with a purpose — not chaos, but order for His people. How humbled we should be to know that he knows and cares about each one of us.

Psalm 103:14 says, "He knows how we are formed, he remembers that we are dust." He knows how weak and powerless we are as human beings. In our natural state we are prone to sin. Even in the forgiven state we are tempted and make mistakes sometimes. Here, then, is where the Holy Spirit takes over with ". . . groans that words cannot express." He makes us aware of doing wrong so that our conscience will move us to right the wrong. What has been destroyed through a mistake or sin can become a real means to increase our faith as confession is made.

The idea, "Now I'm in the will of God, now I'm out — now I'm in — now I'm out," is not scriptural. As long as we, as believers, do not deliberately go against God, but truly want in our hearts to belong to and serve and love God, we remain in His will. He will not disinherit us.

When we deliberately and willingly sin and continue in sin, we are not in the will of God but have ourselves chosen to cause God to disinherit us eternally when judgment day is here. How awful!

As long as this earth has people on it, there will be a battle between good and evil, between God and Satan.

Satan hates you . . . . God loves you.
Satan deceives . . . . God is truth.
Satan blinds . . . . God is light.
Satan hinders . . . . God removes.
Satan binds . . . . God looses.
Satan stirs up . . . . God gives peace.
Satan divides . . . . God unites.

Satan destroys . . . . God builds.

Satan wastes . . . . God saves.

Satan causes fear . . . . God gives confidence.

God's will is for us to learn that he can be depended on. He is steady, unchangeable.

Malachi 3:6 — "I the Lord do not change."

Psalm 100:5 — "For the Lord is good and his love endures forever; his faithfulness continues through all generations."

James 1:17 — "Every good and perfect gift is from above, coming down from the Father of the heavenly lights, who does not change like shifting shadows."

Psalm 119:89 — "Your Word, O Lord, is eternal; it stands firm in the heavens."

It is truly assuring and gives confidence to a believer that this God we serve is steadfast and eternal.

The Word is God's will.

John 1:1 — "In the beginning was the Word, and the Word was with God, and the Word was God."

Psalm 119:89 — "your Word, O Lord, is eternal; it stands firm in the heavens."

Psalm 119:97 — "O, how I love your law. I meditate on it all day long."

Psalm 119:104 — "I gain understanding from your precepts."

When we want to understand more of God's will, it will require reading, praying, studying and being obedient to what we already know. It means that we exercise faith, trust and patience with prayer. "Commit your way to the Lord. Delight yourself in the Lord and he will give you the desires of your heart." Psalm 37.

2 Timothy 2:15 reminds us to, "Do your best to present yourself to God as one approved, a workman who does not need to be ashamed and who correctly handles the word of truth."

God's will is for us to surrender every area of our life to him.

Romans 12:1-2 — "Therefore, I urge you, brothers, in view of God's mercy, to offer your bodies as living sacrifices, holy and pleasing to God — which is your spiritual worship. Do not conform any longer to the pattern of this world, but be transformed by the renewing of your mind. Then you will be able to test and approve what God's will is — his good, pleasing and perfect will."

John 7:17 — "If any one chooses to do God's will, he will find out whether my teaching comes from God or whether I speak on my own. He who speaks on his own does so to gain honor for himself, but he who works for the honor of the one who sent him is a man of truth; there is nothing false about him."

The will of God is to give thanks in everything.

1 Thessalonians 5:18 — "In everything give thanks, for this is the will of God concerning you." (KJV) "Give thanks in all circumstances." (NIV)

How do we give thanks in an adverse circumstance? When we love and obey God we are full of joy. God wants us happy. To love and obey means to be thankful. When adversity comes, we continue to love and obey. We give thanks in the adverse situation, knowing it is allowed in order to be helpful to us. It is for our purification and perhaps for those with whom we come in contact. Through it all is victory. God is glorified because we have testified of His love and care for us.

Colossians 4:12 — The prayer of Epaphros was, ". . . that you may stand firm in all the will of God, mature and fully assured."

Colossians 1:9-14 — Paul, in praying for the church at Colosse, asked ". . . God to fill you with the knowledge of his will through all spiritual wisdom and understanding."

Let God's will control our lives. He gives us enlightenment in the Word if we allow Him to keep us through the Spirit and the Word.

It is the will of God for us to have forgiveness of sins, salvation. It is not God's will to lose a soul to Satan.

If a soul is lost to Satan, it comes about by choice. Not by God's choice, but by a disobedient person's choice.

The whole theme of the Bible is restoration of people to full fellowship with God. We are a part of that theme and plan. When we accept God's plan for our lives and have been 'born again' (born spiritually), we are in God's will. We may not know His full will or plan for us yet, but we go on by faith and trust in His knowledge and care for us, knowing we have the right and privilege not to sin anymore.

It is God's will to do good.

1 Peter 2:15 — "For it is God's will that by doing good you should silence the ignorant talk of foolish men."

Romans 8:28 — "And we know that in all things God works for the good of those who love him, who have been called according to his purpose." Our good and God's good become one, as our aim for doing good is changed. When we need to force ourselves to do good, when we need to stop and think about doing good, we are apt to make excuses about why we cannot or should not. The motive may be wrong.

James 4:17 — "Anyone, then, who knows the good he ought to do and doesn't do it, sins." When we are indwelt with the Spirit of God, love will prompt us. It will move us to do good with the right motives, unselfishly, lovingly and naturally.

When we live in a Christ-honoring way in our daily lives, doing good becomes part of our very existence. We pray to God about our daily living, but God does not need to say to us every morning, "Get up, take a shower, fix breakfast, hoe weeds, feed cattle, plow fields, mend clothing, change diapers, build houses, go to the office, pick up the children from school."

We know how to do these things because He has given us wonderful minds and we are free to make choices in our daily living. God in His omnipotent soverignty gives us the freedom to use self control. We have knowledge about the everyday things of life that are normal because we are created human beings. We continue adding to that knowledge through life's experiences, parenting, study, culture and economics.

There is within a believer, a regenerated spirit of love that helps direct our affairs. Whether our life work is menial service or other service highly regarded by society, we can do it as unto the Lord. We are His people.

Because of the lifestyle we choose, and there are many choices, we assume certain responsibilities. If it is an honorable style, it would be wrong to avoid the normal responsibilities. If it is not honorable, perhaps we need to change the lifestyle or occupation. To do nothing about our responsibilities would please Satan. When our daily responsibilities need to be changed or interrupted at times, the Spirit will help us to know.

God expects us to be morally responsible for what we choose. The spiritual responsibility within our chosen lifestyle is of greatest importance.

Can we be obedient to God where we are? Each of us must answer for ourselves. Does it bring peace?

There may be times when we flounder, trying to know for sure if we are doing God's will.

It is difficult to understand it fully sometimes because we do not see the whole picture. We are not out of God's will because we do not understand. God's plan for our lives may include something quite different from that of our friends, relatives or neighbors, so we cannot draw totally from another person's experience. Both may be in God's will.

The execution of His plan may become evident in different ways so we need to recognize His will in our specific situation and be happy for someone else's recognition in his or her individual situation. God works through our circumstances as we live within His will. He works with individuals.

When a Christian believer is sick or has other adversities, that is not necessarily out of God's will. His permissive will allows these circumstances so that His design or purpose for that individual's life can be accomplished. It may also perhaps be in His design to help those with whom the person comes in contact. All this is done to honor and glorify God in love. 2 Corinthians 1:3-7.

God's love does not jump from one to another in an irresponsible fashion. He loves us, His people, with a steady, everlasting, compassionate, redemptive love as we seek assurance in His will. This develops into trust and hope on our part. It is helpful at times to speak to individual Christian friends or even an entire church group. We need the 'whole council of God.' Prayer is a necessity. When we walk with God every day, the Spirit will help us to receive answers.

We cannot seek from the Spirit things that do not agree with the Word. We need to know God's will. Look into the scriptures, but do it with purpose. Do not just flip your Bible open here and there looking for answers.

I once read a story which illustrates the danger in doing this:

A man let his Bible fall open where it would. He read, "Judas went out and hanged himself." Not satisfied with this passage, he flipped the pages again and read, "Go and do thou likewise." His next flip of pages told him, "What you do, do quickly." To follow those instructions would be folly!

Perhaps some people may find answers by just reading wherever the Bible opens, but usually it is best to use discretion, ask for wisdom, take notes and use helps.

Satan tries and prefers to block our way so we do not or cannot understand the Word. It is very important to be able to converse readily with Jesus anytime. Instead of trying to rebuke Satan, talk to Jesus.

James 4:7 — "Resist the devil and he will flee from you." It is true, we need to resist him, but it is more important to come near to God and He will come near to you.

Don't give Satan the attention he wants. In Revelation 12:10 Satan is called the accuser of the brethren. Sin provides the background for the accusations, while he tries to put guilt upon us. Especially when we are in a weakened condition. Instead of looking over our shoulders all the time to find out if Satan is lurking there, we need to keep our eyes and thoughts on Christ. Let God take charge and Satan will flee.

We have our place here as God's children in His will. We do not want to be crowded out. God's will is to have His people carry on the work that Jesus left for them when he ascended to the Father. The work is to testify for Him so men will know how to be saved, when they are sick or when they are well. God is in control!

The disciples considered it a great privilege that God entrusted them with the Gospel. To have God allow this was most humbling, but very rewarding.

1 Thessalonians 2:3, 4 — "For the appeal we make does not spring from error or impure motives, nor are we trying to trick you. On the contrary, we speak as men approved by God to be entrusted with the gospel. We are not trying to please men but God, who tests our hearts."

There is no mystery or fear in knowing the will of God. it is helpful to know His will. The child of God will then serve Him gladly with obedience, love and faith. We will to do His will.

And he saw the Spirit
of God descending like
a dove.

Chapter XIV
The Holy Spirit

To understand the Holy Spirit, it will be necessary to refer to scriptures that apply to the Holy Spirit and the will of God. Faith and prayer are also intertwined in the references. When some verses are used more than once, consider it extra emphasis. It will help to understand their role in the total healing of a person. It can give a calm assurance to a person who is sick or well or when adversities come.

The subject of the Holy Spirit is a solemn one, but it is also a blessed one. He is such an essential part of a Christian believer's life. He is the part of God that God wants His children to have at all times wherever they are.

The Spirit works as a communication assistant. It is part of God's plan to enter into our experiences. Through the Spirit this can be accomplished.

In the first book of the Bible, Genesis 1:1, 2, we read, "The Spirit of God was hovering over the waters." This was during God's creation time and the first time the Spirit is mentioned. We learn by reading the Bible that the Spirit was working all through the Old Testament scriptures.

"The Spirit in the Old Testament is God active as creator, controller, revealer, quickener, and enabler; and in all this God makes himself present to men in the dynamic demanding way in which the Lord Jesus is now made present to Christian believers today," said J. I. Packer in *Keep in Step With the Spirit*.

In the New Testament the Spirit is mentioned often as a real person to a believer. He is someone with whom we can have close contact. He is one of God's mysteries, a blessed one. The Spirit is definitely not just an influence or force. In John 3:5-7 Jesus told Nicodemus, a seeker of truth, "I tell you the truth, unless a man (person) is born of water (baptized) and the Spirit he cannot enter the kingdom of God. Flesh gives birth to flesh but the Spirit gives birth to Spirit. You must be born again.'' We must have a second birth which is spiritual.

Acts 2:38, 39 mentions two conditions required for receiving the Spirit. "Repent and be baptized every one of you, in the name of the Lord Jesus Christ so that your sins may be forgiven. And you will receive the gift of the Holy Spirit.''

The two conditions are:

1) Repent — a change of mind and heart.

2) Be baptized — an outward expression of an inward cleansing.

Two gifts mentioned in the same verses are that we:

1) Receive forgiveness.

2) Receive the Holy Spirit.

Jesus Christ our Lord offers both.

In 2 Corinthians 9:5 the Spirit is called "God's indescribable gift." A gift from God given so freely to persons who recognize their lost and hopeless condition in their sinful state, and then confess their sin and accept Jesus as the only Saviour and mediator between themselves and God. 1 Timothy 1:5 also discusses this. The promise will be kept. The Holy Spirit will be given.

Jesus faced the challenge of the cross by His obedience to His heavenly Father. He was victor over death and the grave. Glory be to God! Indescribable!

Jesus told his disciples in John 14, "In my Father's house are many mansions (or rooms); if it were not so, I would have told you. I am going there to prepare a place for you. And if I go and prepare a place for you I will come back and take you to be with me that you also may be where I am." He also said the classic, heartwarming words, "I will not leave you as orphans. I will ask the Father and he will give you another counselor to be with you forever, the Spirit of truth." In the absence of the bodily, fleshly Jesus, the Spirit will be a constant presence in us.

In John 14:25-28 Jesus also said, ". . . the Holy Spirit, whom the Father will send in my name, will teach you all things and will remind you of everything I have said to you . . . . If you loved me, you would be glad that I am going to the Father, for the Father is greater than I.''

The Spirit also does more. John 16:7-13 says, ''I tell you the truth. It is for your good that I am going away. Unless I go away the Counselor will not come to you; but if I go, I will send him to you. When he comes, he will convict the world of guilt in regard to sin and righteousness and judgment; in regard to sin, because men do not believe in me; in regard to righteousness, because I am going to the Father where you can see me no longer; and in regard to judgment, because the prince of this world now stands condemned. I have much more to say to you, more than you can now bear.'' This is a sweet, comforting statement telling us how compassionate Jesus is. He makes life bearable for His children as they move forward in faith and obedience, allowing the Spirit freedom to work.

Jesus continues in John 16, ''. . . When he, the Spirit of truth comes, he will guide you into all truth. He will not speak on his own; he will speak only what he hears, and he will tell you what is yet to come. He will bring glory to me by taking from what is mine and making it known to you. All that belongs to the Father is mine. That is why I said the Spirit will take from what is mine and make it known to you.''

''He will not speak on His own; he will only speak what he hears, and he will tell you what is yet to come.

He will bring glory to me by taking from what is mine and making it known to you. All that belongs to the Father is mine. That is why I said the Spirit will take from what is mine and make it known to you.''

— Jesus

This is such a tremendous relationship for a follower of Christ. It is almost overwhelming just to think it through. The Spirit is so alive to us but he does not want anyone to worship him. He wants people to focus on Christ Jesus. He gives out the knowledge of Christ our Lord to the glory of God.

The Holy Spirit is the power that enables a believer to testify for Jesus. In Acts 1:6-8 and Luke 24:49 Jesus told the apostles before His ascension to heaven, "You are witnesses of these things (concerning Jesus) and I am going to send you what my Father promised; but stay in the city until you have been clothed with power from on High." They were to be completely covered and indwelt by the Spirit.

Acts 2:1-4 says the promised Spirit appeared in an upper room of a house in Jerusalem as the apostles waited and prayed. "Suddenly a sound like the blowing of a violent wind came from heaven and it filled the whole house where they were sitting. They saw what seemed to be tongues of fire that separated and came to rest on each of them. All of them were filled with the Holy Spirit and began to speak in other tongues (languages) as the Spirit enabled them."

Acts 2:32-36. Peter, an apostle of Jesus, was testifying for Jesus at Jerusalem. Because everyone in the crowd heard it in his own language, they needed an explanation. He said, "God has raised this Jesus to life, and we are all witnesses of the fact. Exalted to the right hand of God, He has received from the Father the promised Holy Spirit and has poured out what you now see and hear." It was a demonstration of the exalted Christ Jesus pouring out the Spirit. Verse 36 says, "Therefore let all Israel be assured of this: God has made this Jesus, whom you crucified, both Lord and Christ."

"This which you see and hear" was the result of Christ's exaltation or elevation to the highest position and glorification in heaven at the right hand of God.

His promise was kept. This was the miracle of Pentecost. Pentecost stems from a Jewish feast, and just as the appearance of God on Mount Sinai was the birthday of the Jewish nation, so was Pentecost and the coming of the Spirit the birthday of the Christian church.

The Holy Spirit was not given then or now to prove how good or great we are, but to prove the greatness and faithfulness of this exalted Christ Jesus.

Watchman Nee said it well in the book, *The Normal Christian Life*. "Because Jesus died on the cross we have received forgiveness of sins; because He conquered death by His resurrection we have new life in Him; because He was exalted to the right hand of the Father we have received the outpoured Spirit."

The purpose of "this which you now see and hear" was to prove the Lordship of Christ. Too often we fail to realize the great change that came about because Jesus ascended to the Father. Through this He was positively identified on the earth and on the throne as the one with dominion and power, absolute lordship.

The demonstration of the visible tongues of fire does not appear today; and not always does the speaking in other tongues. Tongues are a special gift of the Spirit to be given as He determines or enables people. It is not right to say that a person does not have the Spirit if he does not speak in tongues, because speaking in tongues is a gift of the Holy Spirit and not for man to give. 1 Corinthians 12 lists some spiritual gifts. Read also Romans 12 and Hebrews 2:4. These gifts are given individually and not every person need have all of them. These gifts differ from the fruit of the Spirit.

In Galatians 5:22, 23 (NIV) the fruit of the Spirit is listed as " . . . love, joy, peace, patience, kindness, goodness, faithfulness, gentleness and self-control (or temperance, KJV). Against such things there is no law." The law cannot control you for practicing the production of this fruit.

Jesus said in John 15:8, "This is to my Father's glory that you bear much fruit, showing yourselves to be my disciples." All Christians should have fruit characteristics when they are well or when they are sick or suffering in other ways. Fruit is a sign of spiritual growth.

Psalms 1:2, 3 says

> *"But his delight is in the law of the Lord,*
> *and on His law he meditates day and night.*
> *He is like a tree planted by streams of water,*

which yields its fruit in season
and whose leaf does not wither.
Whatever he does prospers. "

This means the believer grows stronger in his Godly life.

Matthew 7:18-20, "A good tree canot bear bad fruit, and a bad tree cannot bear good fruit. Every tree that does not bear good fruit is cut down and thrown into the fire. Thus, by their fruit you will recognize them."

John 15:4, 5 says, "Remain in me and I will remain in you. No branch can bear fruit by itself; it must remain in the vine. Neither can you bear fruit unless you remain in me. I am the vine; you are the branches. If a man remains in me and I in him, he will bear much fruit; apart from me you can do nothing."

Bearing fruit is very important for the growth of Christians. They can bear fruit according to the way they allow the Spirit to control their lives and work within the framework of the gifts they are given, whether natural or supernatural.

The Holy Spirit sets in motion God's power in our lives.

He is the living presence of God that indwells the hearts of repentant believers. We must believe this to live victoriously. 1 Corinthians 6:19 says, "Do you not know that your body is a temple of the Holy Spirit, who is in you, whom you received from God? You are not your own; you were bought at a price (The blood of Jesus). Therefore honor God with your body." This means when we are sick or when we are well.

The town authorities and the temple priests in Acts 4 wanted to know by what power and name Peter and John were doing good works and preaching. The priests recognized a power they did not know. A believer must also recognize this power to be an effective witness for Christ.

The Spirit is the power behind the men who wrote the Bible.

2 Peter 1:21 says, "For the prophecy came not in old time by the will of man; but holy men of God spake as they were moved by the Holy Ghost." (KJV), or "For prophecy never

had its origin in the will of man, but men spoke from God as they were carried along by the Holy Spirit." (NIV)

The Spirit is a sanctifier.

In Romans 15:16 Paul recognized himself "to be a minister of Christ Jesus to the gentiles with the priestly duty of proclaiming the Gospel of God, so that the Gentiles might become an offering, acceptable to God, sanctified by the Holy Spirit." We become one of God's called out ones, His children by adoption when we accept His plan of salvation. We are sanctified (set apart or made holy) by the Spirit.

2 Timothy 2:21 says, "If a man cleanses himself from evil he will be a vessel unto honor, sanctified or made holy, useful to the Master, and prepared to do every good work." Hebrews 2:11 says, "Both the one who makes men holy (sanctifies) and those who are made holy (sanctified) are of the same family. So Jesus is not ashamed to call them brothers." This is possible because He sent us the Spirit. Romans 8:12-17 says, ". . . the Spirit Himself testifies with our spirit that we are God's children. Now if we are God's children, then we are heirs of God and co-heirs with Christ, if indeed we share in His sufferings in order that we may also share in His glory."

> **Either a well person or a sick person can be an heir with Christ when he is God's child.**

This is a marvelously, overwhelming, humbling, sought-after position for a Christian believer. At least if we understand the full impact of those words. Either a well person or a sick person can be an heir with Christ when he is God's child.

The Spirit fills hearts with love.

Romans 5:5 says, "And hope does not disappoint us because God has poured out His love into our hearts by the Holy spirit, whom He has given us." We too can express love unselfishly, compassionately, and share with Jesus in this way because of the indwelling Spirit.

1 John 4:7-21 says, ". . . If anyone acknowledges that Jesus is the Son of God, God lives in him and he in God. And so we know and rely on the love God has for us. God is love. Whoever lives in love lives in God, and God in him.

The Spirit helps us in our infirmities.

Romans 8:26 says, "In the same way the Spirit helps us in our weakness. We do not know what we ought to pray, but the Spirit Himself intercedes for us with groans that words cannot express." We can ask for help and the Spirit responds in love as we pray to the Father. The Spirit intercedes for us in accordance with God's will. Verse 27.

The Holy Spirit can be grieved.

Ephesians 4:30 says, "And do not grieve (hurt) the Holy Spirit of God with whom you were sealed for the day of redemption."

Grieve is a love word. The Holy Spirit loves us just as Christ does. Romans 15:30 says, "Now I urge you brethren, by our Lord Jesus Christ and by the love of the Spirit, to strive together with me in your prayers to God for me."

We may hurt or anger a person who has no affection for us, but we can grieve only a person who really loves us. We grieve and make the Spirit sad when we get angry or hate in an unhealthy, unloving way. When we wish 'dirt' or 'bad things' for someone else, or have an 'I don't care what happens to him' attitude, or have malice toward anyone, it breeds hatred.

Hate is like a malignancy which grows and threatens our health. The malignancy must be removed or shrunk in size to disappear if possible. Hatred must be removed by forgiveness. Nobody wants to admit to having real hatred, so it rages beneath the surface and infects our relationships until they scorch or turn to rot.

If only we could or would say, "Forgive me, or I am sorry. I did wrong." or "I forgive you for doing wrong." Then physical and spiritual health would improve and the Spirit and the Lord would be pleased.

Forgiving, or asking for forgiveness is not a sign of weakness. It is sometimes hard to do. But if a grievance is just covered over and left to simmer, care must be taken and lovingly exercised lest both persons involved perish. We can sometimes be angry at a deed without being angry at the person who does it.

We also grieve the Spirit when we are otherwise disobedient, when we doubt or act hypocritically, if we are bitter about our condition whether it is good or bad, when we act divisively or by just being unloving. He cannot extend His grace at a time like that and cannot work. God is not pleased. Joy is gone until confession and repentance take place.

The Spirit must not be quenched.

1 Thessalonians 5:19 says, "Quench not the Spirit." "Do not put out His fire or energy. We can quench Him by acting unkindly or criticizing someone who may be delighting in a new spiritual experience. A fire goes out when the fuel supply is withdrawn," Billy Graham says in his book, *The Holy Spirit*. "We smother the fire and may put it out when we belittle the work of others by careless or inappreciative words."

This often happens "when a fresh, new or different movement of the Spirit of God threatens us because the people do not use the old, traditional methods in proclamation or service." Even well-meaning Christians sometimes seek to block what God may be doing in a new way. This blocking opposes God. It smothers or quenches the fire of the Spirit.

This is a serious matter!

We must be honest in asking ourselves if we could be guilty. We need to give this careful attention. The Spirit and the Word always agree and we can be secure in this truth. They agree with the Son and the heavenly Father. We cannot claim the Spirit unless we know His source.

If we have in any way or sense quenched or grieved the Spirit of God or are doing so now, we must not delay in confessing it to God. To delay will add to our sorrow and unhappiness. We must read the Word and repent. Joy will follow.

Quenching the Spirit and grieving the Spirit are sins that a Christian commits. This is painful for the Spirit, but he loves us and draws us back to God.

Blasphemy is something an unbeliever does and is the only unforgivable sin mentioned in the Bible. Matthew 12:31, 32 cautions against this unpardonable sin. Also, in Mark 3:29, we are told, "But whoever blasphemes against the Holy Spirit will never be forgiven; he is guilty of an eternal sin."

Blasphemy is a willful state of the heart and mind.

Blasphemy takes the works of God and the Holy Spirit and falsely attributes them to the power of Satan. By calling good evil and evil good, the conscience becomes dead. When the conscience is killed, there is no more fear of committing blasphemy. To continue resisting Jesus as a Saviour can or may also result in balsphemy and damnation. So often we procrastinate. We delay what we know we should do. That can be disastrous. We become hardened and then impenitent.

When persons are in a weakened physical condition or having other problems, they may believe they have committed the unpardonable sin. They mull over and over 'Why, why, why me?' I only mention this because this kind of fear could develop into a dangerous condition and it is entirely unnecessary. The very fact that they fear they have committed blasphemy is evidence that they have not done so. Trust God completely and fears will vanish. The conscience is alive.

Romans 8:8, 9 says, "Those controlled by the sinful nature cannot please God. You (believers), however, are controlled not by the sinful nature but by the Spirit, if the Spirit of God lives in you. And if anyone does not have the Spirit of Christ, he does not belong to Christ." The very sin of unbelief and not confessing that Jesus came in the flesh already condemns a person when well or sick, rich or poor, full of good works or evil works. Read 1 John 4.

The Spirit cannot be bought.

Acts 8:9-21 says Simon the sorcerer tried to buy the Spirit. We must never try to imitate the Spirit with secular means or use the gifts of the Spirit for our own use or secular advantage. They are spiritual gifts. Jesus acknowledged the Spirit's power in Luke 4:18, 19. "The Spirit of the Lord is upon me because He has anointed me to preach good news to the poor. He has sent me to proclaim freedom for the prisoners (those bound in sin by Satan), and recovery of sight for the blind, to release the oppressed, to proclaim the year of the Lord's favor." This means the fulfillment of Christ's salvation is now here. Christ has come!

The Spirit is a living presence of God in a believer's heart.

He is not visible but is known by His directives, comfort and help to us. When Jesus prayed for God to give us the Spirit, He said in John 14:16, 17, "I will ask the Father, and he will give you another Counselor to be with you forever, the Spirit of truth." God intends to keep us. John 10:27-30 says, "My sheep (Christian believers) listen to my voice; I know them and they follow me. I give them eternal life and they shall never perish; no one can snatch them out of my hand. My Father who has given them to me is greater than all; no one can snatch them out of my Father's hand. I and the Father are one." The Spirit agrees. When His sheep are lost, they themselves have caused the loss and quenched and grieved the Holy Spirit of God. To those who obey and follow, the promise of safety is sure.

In Ephesians 1:13, 14, we read, "And you also were included in Christ when you heard the word of truth, the gospel of your salvation. Having believed, you were marked in him with a seal, the promised Holy Spirit, who is a deposit guaranteeing our inheritance until the redemption of those who are God's possession — to the praise of His glory."

In ancient days and even in modern days, certain documents or parcels are sealed with a waxed, marked seal declaring ownership rights. If the seal is broken before it reaches the right person, it has lost its intended trust in agreement.

So it is with the seal of the Spirit.

When sinners repent, they accept Jesus as their Saviour and are blessed with the gift of the Holy Spirit as a seal to the commitment. Usually water baptism follows and the person is received into the body of believers, the body of Christ the church. Because the Spirit is faithful and does His work, the church will never perish. Our inheritance with Jesus is guaranteed as Jesus promised.

But deliberate, willful, individual or group disobedience with a continuing in sin, will break the seal of the Spirit. Being in this state is horrible. 2 Peter 2:20, 21 says when someone has once known Jesus as Lord and then again becomes entangled in sin, ". . . they are worse off at the end than they were at the beginning."

Jeremy Taylor described the downward progress of an apostate (one who forsakes his faith) this way, "First it startles him, then it becomes pleasing, then delightful, then frequent, then habitual, then confirmed, then he is impenitent, then obstinate, then resolved never to repent, then damned." (*Introduction to Theology*, J. C. Wenger). This again is true when we are sick or when we are well.

We have God's promise and seal of ownership, which will never be broken as long as we abide in Him. "He will never leave us or forsake us." Hebrews 13:5.

1 Corinthians 10:13 says, "No temptation has seized you except what is common to man. And God is faithful; he will not let you be tempted beyond what you can bear. But when you are tempted, he will also provide a way out so that you can stand up under it." The Spirit is the way out as we yield to Him. He works for us.

Questions often are asked about 'Holy Spirit baptism,' 'receiving the Spirit' and 'fullness of the Spirit.' I believe these three terms all signify the same thing.

This is where true faith enters. The Bible says that we receive forgiveness of sins because Jesus shed His blood for mankind. Hebrews 9:22 is clear when it says, "Apart from shedding of blood there is no remission of sins." We need only to grasp this truth and accept it by faith because the Word is truth.

Jesus was crucified and has forgiven our sins by this tremendous act of love, not because of anything good that we do. Going to church, praying often, reading the Bible, paying taxes, helping our neighbor, being kind are all good, but His blood paid the price for us and that satisfied God.

The same would then be true with the receiving of the Holy Spirit.

It is not because of what we have done or do that we receive the Spirit, but because Christ was exalted in heaven.

"Is it possible that Jesus shed His blood for us and we have no forgiveness? NO! Neither is it possible that Christ Jesus has been exalted at the right hand of God and we have not received the gift of the Holy Spirit." (*The Normal Christian Life*, Watchman Nee.) The Spirit baptism would then take place at the time of true conversion; the time when a person makes a commitment to Jesus as his Saviour and Lord of his life.

A new believer is not left alone to flounder. When Christ was exalted, He poured out His Spirit upon us to serve in our hearts as a living presence of God. So why do people keep on praying for what is already theirs? Perhaps it is a lack of full surrender, or lack of experience in faith and experience in God's promises of being trustworthy.

I cannot emphasize too strongly to believe in Him! Accept His promise of Glory for Him and the Spirit for us!

Water baptism signifies:

— A confession of faith in Christ.

— An inward purification or cleansing of the soul from sin.

— A death to sin and Satan's world system and a new life in righteousness with God.

Romans 6:3-11 says, ". . . all of us who were baptized into Christ Jesus were baptized into his death. We were therefore buried with him through baptism into death in order that, just as Christ was raised from the dead through the glory of the Father, we too may live a new life . . . . Now if we died with Christ, we believe that we will also live with him. For we know that since Christ was raised from the dead, he cannot die again;

172

death no longer has mastery over him. The death he died, he died to sin once for all; but the life he lives, he lives to God. In the same way, count yourselves dead to sin but alive to God in Christ Jesus.''

When we are alive to God in Christ Jesus, it is because the Holy Spirit has been sent to us when Jesus went to heaven. We cannot put to death again the ascended Son of God! We can, through God and His Word, ''. . . know Christ and the power of his resurrection and the fellowship of sharing in his sufferings, becoming like him in his death.'' Philippians 3:10, 11. Believe it!

Ephesians 4:1-7 says, ''. . . just as you were called to one hope when you were called. One Lord, one faith, one baptism, one God and Father of all, who is over all, and through all and in you all.''

There may be disagreements about the baptism of the Spirit and about water baptism. This should not lessen our love for each other and God. How could a person receive baptism in the names of the Father, Son and Holy Spirit unless the Holy Spirit was sent after Jesus ascended to the Father. It is a constant relationship.

Special manifestations of the Spirit may come into the category of experience. We experience counseling, comforting, encouraging, directing, edifying, expressing joy and praise. Rather than calling it a baptism, we recognize it as a part of growth and blessing in our experience.

When we are buried with Him in baptism one time, we can hardly be buried again and again. Neither can we be resurrected again and again. As we grow and mature in our Christian lives, we pray in the Spirit. The Holy Spirit's power witnesses of His presence in us, that we are the children of God through Jesus Christ. We seek Him and He causes us to surrender more of ourselves. The power of the Spirit is released in many and varied experiences. Then is when joy can come in its fullness. The more real joy we experience the less we grieve the Spirit.

In Matthew 28:18-20 Jesus gave the disciples a great commission, ''All authority in heaven and earth has been given to me. Therefore, go and make disciples of all nations, baptizing them in the name of the Father and of the Son and of the Holy Spirit, teaching them to obey everything I have commanded you. And surely I will be with you always, to the very end of the age."

1 Corinthians 12:13 says, "For by one Spirit we were all baptized into one body. Acts 2:4 says about the believers at Pentecost, "And they were all filled with the Holy Spirit."

When Saul was blinded, God sent Ananias to him. Ananias said, "Brother Saul, the Lord Jesus has sent me that you might regain your sight and be filled with the Holy Spirit." This was receiving time for healing and the Spirit.

John 3:34 says, "For the one whom God has sent speaks the words of God; to him God gives the Spirit without limit." From this limitless supply every Christian can stay filled.

In his book, *Introduction to Theology*, J. C. Wenger explains, ". . he doesn't need more Spirit but needs a fuller yielding of his own will to God; we need to continually keep every area of our personality and lives open for inspection and sanctification of the Spirit."

To surrender our lives would definitely be a conscious act on our part in obedience to the Word of God.

Some persons may have a vague understanding of the Spirit and His workings. They may not be experiencing fullness of joy and leading a victorious life. They may not recognize Him as an indwelling presence. They will never know great joy until they open their lives to receive all the truth. Jesus says, "Ask, that your joy might be full."

Every Christian believer should want his life to be invaded by the Spirit of God in every area. When we once realize that we have nothing to be ashamed of and embarrassed about to be known as a Christian; when we realize that He is actually with us all the time to help, comfort, guide, teach and love us, we find real assurance and gain confidence as we abide in Him when we are sick or well.

Jesus said in John 8:31-36, "If ye continue in my word then are ye my disciples indeed; And ye shall know the truth and the truth shall make you free . . . . If the Son therefore shall make you free, ye shall be free indeed." (KJV) The freedom or liberty we have depends wholly on obedience. Jesus asks that we continue, or abide in His Word. This is the price of freedom.

2 Corinthians 3:17, 18 says, "Now the Lord is the Spirit, and where the Spirit of the Lord is, there is freedom." The spirit promises freedom! He gives liberty from the slavery of sin when we are well or sick. Liberty and peace join together in Christ. Verse 18, "And we who with unveiled faces all reflect the Lord's glory are being transformed into His likeness with ever-increasing glory, which comes from the Lord, who is the Spirit."

God is still in the process of creating. His indwelling Spirit is so vital in this creation process. Man was created in God's image but through sin that image was marred. Because of the ascended Jesus Christ our Lord and the out-poured indwelling Holy Spirit God can recreate us. Recreate us to reproduce the life of Christ and be conformed into His image. Praise His name!

We can have constant access to God and "He having begun a good work in us will carry it on to completion until the day of Jesus Christ." Philippians 1:6. Take time here and read 2 Corinthians 4.

Reference Guide

God, the Holy Spirit

1. Genesis 1:2 . . . . the Spirit hovered over the unformed world.
2. John 14:16-18, 24, 26 . . . He is another Comforter and a Teacher.
3. John 6:63 . . . . He makes us alive.
4. John 16:13 . . . . He is the Spirit of Truth.
5. John 16:8 . . . . He reproves the world of sin.
6. John 3:6 . . . . Man is born of the Spirit when he becomes a Christian believer.
7. John 3:34 . . . . The Spirit is given without measure.
8. John 15:26 . . . . He will testify of Jesus.
9. 1 John 4:1-4 . . . . Greater is He (Spirit) that is in you than he that is in the world.
10. 1 Corinthians 3:16 . . . . . . Your body is the temple for the Spirit.
11. 1 Corinthians 6:19 . . . . . . Your body is the dwelling place for the Spirit.
12. Hebrews 10:15 . . . . The Spirit is witness to a believer's sanctification.
13. Romans 5:5 . . . . The love of God is spread by the Spirit.
14. Romans 8:14-16 . . . . He motivates believers and gives them assurance.

Who May And May Not Receive The Holy Spirit

1. Luke 11:13 . . . . Those who ask for Him.
2. Acts 2:38 . . . . A penitent believer.
3. Galatians 3:5, 13, 14 . . . . Those who accept Jesus Christ by faith.
4. Acts 5:32 . . . . Those who obey Him.
5. John 14:16 . . . . Those for whom Christ intercedes.
6. Acts 8:14-17 . . . . Gentiles receive the Spirit; Simon the Sorcerer does not.
7. Acts 5:3, 4 . . . . Ananias and Sapphira lie to Him and die.

Symbols Of The Spirit

1. John 3:5-7, 22, 23 . . . . . . Water.
2. Isaiah 4:4, 5 . . . . Fire.
3. Matthew 3:11 . . . . Fire.
4. 1 John 2:20, 27 . . . . Oil/anointing.
5. Hebrews 1:9 . . . . Oil of Joy.
6. Acts 2:2-11 . . . . Wind and Tongues of Fire.
7. Ezekiel 37:9-14
   Acts 2:2 . . . . Wind.
8. Matthew 3:16
   John 1:32-34 . . . . Dove.
9. Isaiah 6:8
   Luke 9:34-36
   Mark 9:7-8 . . . . Voice.
10. Acts 13:2 . . . . Voice.
11. John 16:13 . . . . Truth.
12. Ephesians 4:30 . . . . Seal.
13. 2 Corinthians 1:22 . . . . . . Seal.

The Fruit Of The Spirit — Galatians 5:22, 23

Fruit	Further Reference
1. Love	1 John 4:11 — Beloved, if God so loved us we ought also to love one another.
2. Joy	Philippians 1:2 — Fulfill ye my joy.
3. Peace	Philippians 4:7 — Peace that passes understanding.
4. Longsuffering	Ephesians 4:2 — Forbearing one another (patience).
5. Gentleness	Ephesians 4:32 — Be ye kind one to another.
6. Goodness	Romans 15:14 — Full of goodness.
7. Faith	1 John 5:4 and Ephesians 2:8 — Victory overcomes the world.
8. Meekness	Matthew 5:5 — Blessed are the meek.
9. Temperance	1 Corinthians 9:5 — Everyone who strives for the mastery is temperate in all things.

Three In One — A Triune God

1. Isaiah 9:6, 7	The Son and Spirit recognized in God.
2. Matthew 3:16, 17	At Jesus' baptism.
3. Luke 3:22	At Jesus' baptism.
4. John 1:32, 34	At Jesus' baptism.
5. Matthew 28:19	The great commission; go ye and baptize.

An almighty God is our Father, our Friend, our Comforter, our Guide, our Motivator, our All in All when we are sick or well, happy or sad, rich or poor, any color or race. We praise and thank Him forevermore.

May God himself, the God
of peace, sanctify you
through and through,

May your whole spirit,
soul and body be kept
blameless at the coming
of our Lord Jesus Christ,
The one who calls you is
faithful and he will
do it.

I Thessalonians 5:23

Chapter XV
Thy Will Be Done

We have taken a closer look at many examples of different kinds of adversity and illness. Adversity, pain and suffering are part of God's present plan for His children. We must be careful in asking for healing so that His will be done and the Father be glorified.

When it is not in his immediate plan, He will supply sufficient grace and perhaps make His will known another time or in another way. If it is not instant or when we wish it, we need not be discouraged. Discouragements usually come because we do not get our own way and in our own time.

We need to be faithful, joyful, patient and content, continuing to be obedient and faithful in using our time as an opportunity for good. Sometimes the attitude people have during sickness or other adversity will indicate how spiritually their life is being lived. God alone knows what lies ahead if restoration is effected by demand for selfish reasons.

Will there be: joys . . . . heartaches?
wholeness . . . . depression?
blessing . . . . cursing?
peace . . . . trials?

We must always pray in faith, believing according to God's will. Always say, "Thy will be done." A ripe seasoned faith will say, "Thy will be done." A person with an immature faith, although wanting to do right but confused about asking things of God may say, "Please, God, do it." They insist for selfish reasons.

Sometimes people insist it is God's will for us to be well all the time. Why not believe that God is able to keep us well. Very simple! No doubt about it! He is able! This is faith and truth! This is using wisdom and understanding. Let us not make God small. He may allow difficulties, but He is able to keep us.

Solomon in Proverbs 4 talks about the importance of getting wisdom and understanding and using it right. Verse 7 says, "Wisdom is supreme: therefore get wisdom. Though it cost all you have, get understanding." When read correctly in context, Verse 22 says it contributes to the wholeness of a person.

In Daniel 3 the story of the three Hebrew men in a fiery furnace is a good example of putting complete trust of our lives in God's control. They said, "Our God can deliver us, but if He does not, what difference does it make?" They were resigned to do God's will and He did save them. We have all these valid records which we can believe by faith. They are good today as well as they were then.

In John 10:25 Jesus answered the Jews question, "Are you the Messiah?" with "I told you and you believed not." And to the disciples in 14:11 He said, "Believe me for the very work's sake." All the healing that was done was to confirm faith, the word, or identify Jesus, or to reveal glory or glorify God, show mercy, compassion, or love. Never was it done for a show or entertainment, never for finances, fake representations, undue publicity, fund raising compaigns or healing campaigns.

Some persons involved in physical healing campaigns want us to believe that if there is no healing, a person has not enough faith. It is a sin to be sick, they say.

Is this consistent? Are the people making these claims found doing work in nursing homes where many strong in faith live? Do they nonselectively work in hospitals? Do they visit crippled children's homes, mental hospitals, criminally insane institutions? Why not? Should their own faith not be sufficient for one as well as the other?

Sometimes they emphasize physical healing in such a way that it would be a necessary part of salvation. This cannot be true! "For whosoever shall call upon the name of the Lord (confess their sin and acknowledge Jesus) shall be saved." Romans 10:13

When healing does not take place after persons have been exposed to these dramatic healing services or campaigns, they often become disillusioned and lose their spiritual way. They even blame other people. They may believe God does not love them so He did not heal. A real depression may set in. It is a contradiction to faith. To believe in this kind of healing is not a condition for salvation. Many times these healers use words to heal people they do not know individually. They often work enmasse or in groups, which is no condemnation. Evangelization does bring changes. But when physical signs or changes are emphasized more than the Physician God, the miracle becomes a problem when we are well or sick.

Nowhere in the scriptures is good health set aside as a special sign of God accepting us as His children.

Jesus was interested in the whole person, not just in the physical. In fact, the physical seems to be secondary in importance. Even though He had the power to heal en masse, He chose to do it individually except in the case of the 10 lepers.

James 5 says the prayer of faith shall save the sick. Is it not true that death is inevitable? Any healing is only temporary! "It is appointed unto man to die once and after that the judgment." Hebrews 9:27.

Death was not natural — but acquired — now natural.

Sin was not natural — but acquired — now natural.

God has put certain powers of healing within a person to fight diseases and sicknesses; a system to even ward off these diseases and sicknesses. But the healing process becomes hindered at times through the natural decaying process. We begin to die, or are subject to die as soon as we are born. Most of us continue to grow and go through a normal maturing process in life.

"Pearls are made when an irritating and painful substance lodges in the living flesh of a shellfish. As the healing processes go on, a pearl is formed." (Clark's Commentary). There are no pearls without pain.

This is what the disciples learned and taught in Acts 14:22. "We must go through many hardships to enter the kingdom of God." Hebrews 12:5-12 talks about the discipline of God's children. "Endure hardships as discipline." Discipline means instruction or teaching, sometimes for correction. It may not be pleasant when we have hardships, but they are necessary for our good, "that we may share in His holiness." The Lord disciplines or teaches those He loves.

John 16:33 says, "In this world you will have trouble. But take heart! I have overcome the world."

1 Peter 5:10 says, "After we have suffered a while God Himself will restore us." Peter refers to suffering for Christ's sake. We begin to suffer for Christ's sake when we ourselves believe and accept His suffering on the cross for our sinful selves, for we were included, but Jesus was our one and only substitute.

The Christian believer, who has in the person of Christ died, ought to have no more to do with sin. We are made to cease from sin. We want to focus on Christ instead of the flesh. In a Christ-like attitude of love toward human needs we suffer with others in their struggle to be set free from sin. Or perhaps their suffering is in another area, even physical. When we can help another person we want to remain faithful no matter what the cost. Even living faithfully for Christ in a world where Satan is allowed to be prince is suffering for Christ. As we suffer for human needs, we become one with Christ in suffering.

Jesus Christ through the cross experience suffered more than any person ever suffered. Isaiah 52:14 says, "His appearance was so disfigured beyond that of any man and His form marred beyond human likeness." Romans 8:18 says, "Our present sufferings are not worthy to be compared with the glory that will be revealed to us." When compared to eternity, and the seeing of God face to face, the sufferings we have now are nothing. No comparison for the glory that will be revealed to us, all because of the sufferings of Jesus on the cross. 1 Peter 2:21 says Christ "suffered as an example."

Many different sufferings, including sickness, have come upon us through the sin of Adam and Eve. In this sense only can we say that sickness comes from Satan. I believe it is right

185

to say it comes because of Satan's deceitfulness, rather than from Satan. We cannot lay the blame on Satan when we are responsible and choose to sin. He is nearby with his temptations and evil deceit, trying to seduce us, but we make the decisions. Satan would like to bear the blame, for he diverts our attention away from God. He must have done his very best in the garden of Eden.

I do not believe Satan has an emotion called love. He is in competition with God who is love; therefore the opposite would be true for Satan. His intent is to oppose and accuse God's very love. He is always in conflict with God.

A Christian may suffer much more than an unbeliever because he suffers for Christ's sake. An unbeliever cannot suffer for Christ's sake. In 2 Timothy 1:7, 8 it says, "God has not given us a spirit of fear but of love." We suffer with Him because we want to love and obey Him; therefore, we can do anything He requires or allows us to do as His children. He will be with us.

When Jesus sent the apostles and an additional seventy-two men to go into more areas to do His work, He gave them discipling lessons. His instructions are given to the apostles in Luke 9:1-10, Matthew 10:1-16 and again later in Matthew 28:19. The seventy-two are sent in Luke 10:1-9. He told them to preach, teach, evangelize, baptize, heal the sick, cleanse the lepers, raise the dead, cast out devils. He warned them that they would be like sheep among wolves and needed to be "shrewd as snakes and as innocent as doves." He also reminded them to depend on the Spirit for what to say. He told them to take no luggage, but to let other people help them with food, clothing and places to rest.

Before Jesus even sent them, He gave them special power for doing His work. They were truly blessed with God's supernatural power of the Spirit for many needs, but could not always use their gifts at their own will. Matthew 17:14-21.

Christian believers today are also blessed with the same power of the Spirit given according to need. Jesus shares this power through the Holy Spirit and he said, "All power is given to me in heaven and on earth." His power can heal or not heal. Luke 9:11 says Jesus healed those that needed healing. It does not say He healed all people everywhere. God's power never diminishes. We can depend on and trust His power. We belong to Him and through Him receive what is for our benefit and His glory.

When the scripture speaks about the gifts of the Spirit, it always refers to gifts of healing. It is always plural. There may be different gifts, then, for healing. Not everyone that has a gift for one would necessarily have a gift for another, but they could have all. The apostles evidently did in those early Christian years.

It would be unwise any time to try to exercise any gift of healing unless one is fully consecrated and in harmony with God through faith in His power and might and wise in discernment. Consider the story of the demons in Chapter VI.

On the positive side, it can be a strengthening time to all concerned when scriptural practices are followed. Only God's power can heal the sick. We have His promise also in Mark 11:24 that, "Whatever you ask for in prayer, believe that you have received it, and it will be yours."

This promise contains two limitations — when we pray and if we believe.

When we talk to God some things we desire just disappear. We sometimes want, but do not need. The realization of this during prayer makes us want what God wants. John 15:7 says, "If you abide in me and my words abide in you, you shall ask what you will and it shall be done unto you." (KJV) Is this an unlimited guarantee? This says it is not what anyone wills, but what is willed by a person "abiding in Christ."

Prayer is so very important. Along with prayer in seeking answers to all the questions about the different ideas about healing, we can use wisdom like Gamaliel did. In Acts 5:34-39 we read that Gamaliel was a council member of the Sanhedrin. He was a teacher of the law and honored by all people. He dealt wisely with the people.

His wisdom was heard when Peter and John were delivered from prison by an angel. After they were seen in public they were recaptured by officers of the law and taken to Gamaliel. There they testified for God. Gamaliel reminded the officers of two different men who met disaster after they by false teachings had drawn many people away from God.

Gamaliel said to the officers, "Leave these men alone! Let them go! For if their purpose or activity is of human origin, it will fail. But if it is from God, you will not be able to stop these men; you will only find yoruselves fighting against God."

An example of this happening today is the poison suicide deaths of hundreds of people who followed Jim Jones' teaching in Guyana during the 1970s. He led many people astray and met disaster. His teaching was false. It failed.

Well-meaning Christians may find themselves fighting against God when they become frustrated and ridicule new activities they believe are not of God. We need to live carefully and unselfishly, allowing the Spirit of God the freedom to work. We need to believe in a God of love and mercy to direct us daily. We need to try to discern what is from God.

In Acts 5:41, Peter and John were not imprisoned after they saw Gamaliel, but they were flogged. They rejoiced because they had been counted worthy of suffering disgrace for the name of God.

In all the healings Jesus did, no one denied the healing. All tried to identify the healer. This is where the controversy began.

Jesus made each work of healing a time for instilling into the mind and heart of the people some spiritual thought or principle. He used earthly blessings to turn the hearts of people to receive spiritual blessings. His real mission was to heal the sin-sick soul.

In Luke 7:18-35 we have the account of John the Baptist in prison soon after he had baptized Jesus. He sent two of his (John's) disciples to find out if the man he had heard rumors about was Jesus the Messiah. Immediately after John had baptized Jesus, Jesus went up into the mountain, where He fasted forty days and was tempted of Satan. When Jesus returned, John had been imprisoned. John wanted to know if Jesus was . . . "the one who was to come, or should we expect someone else?"

In verse 21 it says Jesus first cured many who had diseases, sicknesses and evil spirits, and gave sight to the blind. In verse 22 He told John's disciples to "go back and report to John what you have seen and heard: The blind receive sight, the lame walk, those who have leprosy are cured, the deaf hear, the dead are raised to life and the good news is preached to the poor. Blessed is the man who does not fall away on account of me."

To John was opened the same truth that had come to Elijah in the desert when ". . . a strong wind rent the mountains and brake in pieces the rocks before the Lord . . . then after the fire, a still small voice." 1 Kings 19:11, 12 (KJV).

Jesus did His works not by overthrowing governments and working politically, but by treating human needs in order to establish a heart-relationship with each person, thereby declaring and revealing Himself as the Son of God, their promised Messiah. It is this "still, small voice" we hear now when sickness or other adversity comes to us. It is God's love speaking to us. We can hear this voice any time when we listen, when we are well or sick. This is called normal Christian living.

People are very quick to form opinions about why the righteous get sick or suffer. Job did not know why he suffered in such an unusual way. He did realize that he was small and God was great. He was blessed for his faithfulness.

We also react to loss according to our faith. These losses can be physical conditions, finances, friends or self image.

We need not go around with long faces looking for suffering and persecution. When we are members of the body of Christ we belong to each other although we are separate parts. When one member suffers, the others suffer. When one member rejoices, the others rejoice. This is how it is meant to work. We need to have no guilt if we personally are not afflicted or suffering, but it is important to keep in tune with the other members that belong to Christ. We must live normally and allow the Lord to bring about in His own way and time whatever obedient living calls for in us.

We may never know fully why a particular sickness, suffering or tragedy is allowed for a particular person at a particular time. We can know this — God will never allow more than He and we can bear together. If God's love shows through, it is only a physical limitation or tragedy, not a spiritual loss.

The suffering of Jesus during His preaching years and the weighty suffering on the cross ended in victory by a glorious resurrection and ascension to glory. He made it possible for us to bear what we will bear to fulfill God's plan. He made it affordable for us.

We must live normally and allow God to bring about in His own way and time whatever obedient living calls for in us.

Hebrews 5:8 — "Although He was a Son, He learned obedience from what He suffered."

Philippians 2:8 — ". . . he humbled Himself and became obedient to death — even death on a cross!"

Philippians 1:29 — ". . . it has been granted to you on behalf of Christ . . . to suffer for him."

1 Peter 2:21 — Jesus suffered as an example. Chapter 4 discusses his suffering "in the flesh."

Hebrews 12:4-13 — ". . to endure hardships as discipline."

2 Timothy 4:5 — ". . . endure hardship . . ."

James 5:10, 11 — suffering was sent in compassion and mercy.

Romans 8:16, 17 — "Now if we are God's children, then we are heirs — heirs of God and coheirs with Christ, if indeed we share in his sufferings in order that we may also share in his glory."

2 Timothy 2:12 — "If we endure, we will also reign with Him . . ."

1 Peter 4:13 — "Rejoice that you participate in the sufferings of Christ." Verse 15 says NOT to suffer as a murderer or thief or any other kind of criminal or even as a meddler. Those actions are of Satan's deceitfulness. Verse 16 — Do not be ashamed to suffer as a Christian. But praise God that you bear that name.

Some of these scriptures seem a little difficult to understand until we realize that as we sufer we can relate to the sufferings of Jesus in a much better way. It is God's way to make us sure that we know we can become legitimate subjects to claim our inheritance with Jesus. It is God's will!

By these scriptures and examples, I believe we can safely make some deductions about why the righteous suffer. They are:

1. So the power of God may rest on us to testify of Jesus.

2. Just because we belong to God; He being our Heavenly Father teaches or corrects His children in love, just as an earthly father would do for his children. Always it is for good, never for evil.

3. As an example in faith and patience for better things.

4. So we can share in His heavenly estate.

5. To carry out His plan for us and perhaps those around us, developing our potential and theirs. We must trust His judgment and be faithful and obedient.

6. 1 Peter 1:6, 7 — "In this you greatly rejoice, though now for a little while you may have had to suffer grief in all kinds of trials. These have come so that your faith — of greater worth than gold, which perishes even though refined by fire — may be proved genuine and may result in praise, glory and honor when Jesus Christ is revealed."

We are sometimes unable to find meaning in suffering so we need to trust the Lord.

Why children suffer is difficult to explain, so we leave that with God. When no definite instruction is given, it is better not to speculate or imagine. We leave that responsibility to God.

Revelation 20:12 describes both great and small standing before the throne. Because of the resurrection of Jesus, they will live.

For the unbelievers there can be only one reason for suffering. It is to make them God conscious, so they would perhaps hear the voice of God and repent of their sins.

Isaiah 48:9-11 — God afflicted Israel to refine her and even with all her stubbornness God retains His love for her and retains His glory.

Romans 5 — Suffering produces perseverance and patience. This is a fruit of the Spirit.

Psalm 119:71-75 — David says, "It was good for me to be afflicted so that I could learn your decrees."

If suffering was granted and Jesus is our example, why do I want healing? For my selfish reasons or to testify of God's grace? We all like to be well and energetic and participate in life's activities. God wants us to participate as a whole person. Sometimes one part of the whole needs special attention and we need healing.

Is healing to be done within the framework of the church? That is the scriptural way when divine healing is desired, whether it is physical or spiritual. It could, but it is not stated that it should, involve the whole congregation, except that they are members one of another.

The elders as representatives of the congregation and God, are usually called; the prayer of faith is given, and an anointing with oil is done. People of faith will accept God's will in the matter to heal or not to heal at that time. God uses visible demonstrations sometimes. He would really only need to will it done, but we humans need the relationship of asking and receiving.

There are times when anointing is not appropriate. "The anointing is not for saving souls, not for the unconverted, not for infants, nor for those who have no prayer of faith." (*Doctrines of the Bible*, by Daniel Kauffman.) "If he has committed sins, they shall be forgiven him." James 5:15. This is the Word of God! It is an act of love, and in hope and obedience we need to say "God be glorified!"

When we examine all these records and believe the Bible to be true, we should have no problem with those who teach with seemingly strange and different methods, unless it causes confusion. If they deny the Father and His omnipotence, Christ the Son, The Holy Spirit, Heaven, Hell, or the atonement for sins by Jesus' shed blood on the cross, the Bible says it is wrong.

Sometimes people believe they need to bring something new to Christianity because they believe they have a special revelation. The Bible is the complete revelation of Jesus Christ. Because it is complete, we need not expect to go farther than ". . . the faith that was once for all entrusted to the saints." Jude 3, 4.

These 'new revelations' are often confusing, and have been found to be false. The world is full of false hopes and emotional blind alleys. This is the source of much confusion.

God has use for many different people: the quiet ones, the shouters, watchers, waiters, emotionally expressive or sedate. If they have been "born again" into the family of God and have the Spirit of God in their hearts, they belong to Him.

There is only one Holy Spirit. 1 John 4:1-6 says, "Dear friends, do not believe every spirit, but test the spirits to see whether they are from God, because many false prophets have gone out into the world. This is how you can recognize the Spirit of God: (read carefully)

"Every Spirit that acknowledges that Jesus Christ has come in the flesh is from God, but every spirit that does not acknowledge Jesus, is not from God. This is the spirit of the antichrist which you have heard is coming and even now is already in the world. You, dear children, are from God and have overcome them because the one who is in you is greater than the one who is in the world. They are from the world and therefore speak from the viewpoint of the world, and the world listens to them. We are from God, and whoever knows God listen to us, but whoever is not from God does not listen to us. This is how we recognize the spirit of truth and the spirit of falsehood."

The demonstration of the Spirit of truth, which is the Holy Spirit, may be manifested differently in different people, but never to dishonor God or bring shame to the name of Jesus. Sometimes the 'understanding is darkened' or veiled. Sometimes there is no 'fullness of joy' among people. How do we reflect, or allow the Spirit to reflect Jesus through us? Do we reflect love and light according to God's Word? Do we reflect compassion in a pulled every-which-way world? Do we extend to the world a healing wholeness plan, a recovery plan for the sick and wounded, the destitute and lost, the hungry or those in prison? God's truth will remain as will His love, so we can allow the Spirit to demonstrate this through us when we believe, whether we are sick or well.

1 John 4:11 says, "Beloved, if God so loved us, we ought also to love one another."

Philippians 1:12-30 is Paul's glory in Christ. Read it all. Verse 20, 21 says, "I eagerly expect and hope that I will in no way be ashamed, but will have sufficient courage so that now as always Christ will be exalted in my body, whether by life or by death. For to me to live is Christ and to die is gain."

In conclusion, to those who read this and if you are an unbeliever, confess Christ as Lord of your life. Do not delay. You will have the best friend to help you through tough times and good times. He is faithful!

To the Christian believers. We can have an overwhelming sense of peace to know we belong to the family of God. We can with full confidence entrust our lives into His care and keeping when we are well or when we are sick or have other adversities. We can trust God and His love to do for us what we cannot do for ourselves, knowing it is best for us.

1 John 3:1 says, "Behold, what manner of love the Father has bestowed upon us, that we should be called the children of God."

It is good for us to say aloud, "I am God's child. I love you Lord. Thank you Jesus for saving my soul from eternal death and giving me life in its place." This helps to confirm why we believe what we believe. Let us not make our God incapable of taking care of us.

In Lamentations 3:32, 33 we read, "Though he brings grief, he will show compassion, so great is his unfailing love. For he does not willingly bring affliction or grief to the children of men." God is trustworthy. His grace is sufficient.

When we are well or sick or suffering in any way, we must remember that we have a sovereign Lord God caring for us. We need not fear if He redirects our way sometimes to get us in line with His purposes.

We cannot always see the end from the beginning, so it does not make sense to us each time. We need a closer look.

In Proverbs 19:21 we read, "Many are the plans in a man's heart, but it is the Lord's purpose that prevails."

Again, we come to trusting God in what He has done, is doing and will do. To trust means to rely or depend on Him, have confidence and hope in Him. We believe in Him and the truth of His Word. The Psalmist says in 33:10, 11, "The Lord foils the plans of the nations; he thwarts the purposes of the peoples. But the plans of the Lord stand firm forever, the purposes of his heart through all generations."

I believe the essentials for a healing wholeness are given as the Lord wants me to give them. May they be a blessing to all who read.

We want to remain faithful at all costs. He will keep us in joy, health, sickness or other suffering. We must trust Him. His judgment is right. We are in the process of carrying out His will to His glory and honor and for our eternal rest with Him.

May we bring thanks and praise to our most holy and sovereign God who reigns over His created universe. "Let us fix our eyes on Jesus, the author and perfecter of our faith, who for the joy set before Him, endured the cross, scorning its shame, and sat down at the right hand of the throne of God."

Hebrews 12:2

Praise be to you, O Lord,
God of our father Israel,
from everlasting to everlasting.

Yours, O Lord, is the greatness
    and the power
and the glory and the majesty
    and the splendor,
for everything in heaven
    and earth is yours.

Yours, O Lord, is the kingdom;
    You are exalted as head
    over all.

Works Cited

Bonhoeffer, Dietrich. *The Cost of Discipleship*: The Macmillan Co.

Brand, Dr. Eric and Yancey, Philip. *Fearfully and Wonderfully Made*: Zondervan Publishing House.

Edmond, V. Raymond. *Between Christ and Satan* by Kurt Koch: West Germany and in U.S. by Kregal Publications, by permission.

Graham, Billy. *The Holy Spirit*: Word Books Publishers, by permission.

Koch, Kurt. *Between Christ and Satan*: Kregel Publications.

Kauffman, Daniel. *Doctrines of the Bible*: Herald Press.

Lewis, C. S. *Screwtape Letters*: Time Incorporated.

Maxwell, L. E. *Crowded to Christ*: Wm. B. Eerdmans Pub. Co.

Nee, Watchman. *The Normal Christian Life*: Tyndale House Publishers, Inc., 1977, by permission.

Packer, J. I. *Keep in Step With the Spirit*: Fleming H. Revell Company, by permission.

Wenger, J. C. *Introduction to Theology*: Herald Press.

"Blessed Redeemer," on page 26, copyright 1921 Singspiration Music/ASCAP. All rights reserved. Used by permission of Benson Music Group, Inc.

"Faith Is A Living Power From Heaven," on page 133, and "Praise To The Lord, The Almighty," on page 44, copied from "The Mennonite Hymnal," 1969 by Herald Press, Scottdale, PA 15683. Used by permission.

Mrs. Baer has given us a most extensive study of God's word, the fruit of what has obviously been a labor of love. I am sure it will prove to be a great help to others who, like her, have had to deal with illness and suffering and have had to confront the question "why?"

The treatise she has written leads the reader on a journey through scripture that deals with much more than the meaning of illness and healing. She appropriately helps us understand that wholeness, not perfection, is possible for every Christian, and that wholeness, not necessarily freedom from illness, is God's promise to every believer.

There are 2 particular strengths I see to Mrs. Baer's book. The first is that she is writing out of the context of her personal pilgrimage through pain and disability.

The second are the extensive scriptural citations. There are other books on healing; I've not seen one that leads the reader through such an exhaustive scriptural search.

I appreciated especially her treatment of what it means to pray "in God's name," in His will."

I believe the book's greatest use will be to the one, who, like the author, is wrestling with God over personal illness and is asking "why?" But since it relates this question to the overall meaning of life and of salvation, it will be of help to the well as well as to the unwell, and to Christians in the healing professions.

— Willard S. Krabill, M.D.

Notes

Notes